How to Be
Kind

How to Be Kind

Little Examples of Selflessness and Courtesy

Andrew Taylor

The History Press

For Sam, Abi and Bec
Lucy, Sophie and Tom

First published 2011 under the title *Random Acts of Politeness: Eccentric, Quirky and Occasionally Suicidal Examples of Selflessness and Courtesy*

This paperback edition published 2023

The History Press
97 St George's Place, Cheltenham,
Gloucestershire, GL50 3QB
www.thehistorypress.co.uk

British Library Cataloguing in Publication Data.
A catalogue record for this book is available from the British Library.

ISBN 978 1 80399 483 3

Typesetting and origination by The History Press
Printed and bound in Great Britain by TJ Books Limited, Padstow, Cornwall.

MIX
Paper from
responsible sources
FSC® C111584
www.fsc.org

Trees for LYfe

CONTENTS

INTRODUCTION

Everybody knows, of course, that standards of good manners have declined in recent years. Like the sunnier summers that we used to enjoy, the better music, the funnier jokes and the tastier dinners, this collapse of courtesy becomes increasingly obvious the older and more crotchety we get.

Plenty of the anecdotes in this book seem to support that view. They demonstrate the kindness, consideration and often courage that has been shown in the past by great generals and by ordinary soldiers, by kings and commoners, by people in high society and by very young children.

However, perhaps inconveniently, others will show that precisely the same qualities exist today. By Premiership footballers and international sportsmen, by journalists and television personalities, by the queen herself and from a simple teenage girl writing to her dad: there are contemporary examples of generosity, fellow-feeling, tolerance and decency that stand comparison with anything in the past.

The stories are true, and they come from a wide variety of sources, from our own age and from ancient history. Good manners and courtesy, they say, are not a matter of using the right fork to eat your devilled kidneys, and not much to do with remembering to say 'Please' and 'Thank you'; they are about treating people with unselfishness, sympathy and open-heartedness. Civilisation, perhaps, is a matter of treating people decently.

Often amusing, sometimes moving, occasionally astounding and always fascinating, *How to Be Kind* is both a marvellous read and a tribute to some of the finest, if often overlooked, qualities of humankind.

Here, then, is a celebration of everything that is most noble and selfless in human beings – even if, just occasionally, the reader may be left thinking, 'These people must be barking mad!'

I

SOLDIER, SOLDIER

In the eighteenth century, it must often have seemed as if a degree of lunacy was a necessary prerequisite for success as a military commander. Certainly King George II thought so: told by some of his courtiers that General Wolfe, who had captured the Canadian city of Quebec from the French, was clearly mad, he is said to have retorted, 'Mad, is he? Well, I hope he will bite some of my other generals.'

But that apparent madness could result in exuberant displays of leadership and occasional blistering, reckless bravery and determination. It was an age of aristocratic panache, of extravagant gestures, of brash self-confidence, and of gentlemanly imperturbability under fire.

Perhaps those days are gone: soldiers, after all, no longer march off to war in the bright red uniforms that once made them such a tempting target for enemy riflemen; they no longer fight in smartly drawn-up square formations, firing off regular volleys of musket shot. But the military character has always valued courage, discipline and the readiness to sacrifice oneself for the wider good.

The idea of politeness and *savoir faire* in battle, when groups of men are straining every sinew in an effort to kill each other, may seem grotesque. But many of these stories demonstrate how aristocrats and commanders and ordinary footsoldiers, sailors and airmen alike, throughout history, have shown their true colours and their essential humanity under almost unimaginable pressure.

Some of them may seem barely sane; some show astonishing courage and self-sacrifice; some speak of sensitivity, even gentleness. But they are all stories about the way people can respond to the challenges of war and the danger of imminent death with grace, dignity and courtesy.

After you ...

The Battle of Fontenoy was fought on 11 May 1745, in present-day Belgium, as part of the War of the Austrian Succession. It may be largely forgotten today that it was a French victory over a combined Anglo-Dutch-Hanoverian force, but it is remembered for a bizarre exchange between two rival commanders.

Lord Charles Hay, commanding a detachment of the 1st Foot Guards (now the Grenadier Guards), marched his men to within musket shot of the French *Maison du Roi*, an elite regiment of the royal guards of King Louis XV. Since muskets – although they inflicted terrible injuries – were notoriously inaccurate, that meant they were barely thirty paces from the enemy.

Riding out in front of his troops, Lord Charles raised a silver hip flask towards the French in a mocking toast. '*Messeirs les Gardes Françaises, s'il vous plaît tirez le premier!*' he called out ('Gentlemen of the French Guard, please fire first!'). One sergeant, staring at the levelled muskets of the French, is reported to have said: 'For what we are about to receive, may the Lord make us truly thankful!' But the French commander, the Comte d'Auteroche, was equal to Lord Charles' sangfroid.

'Gentlemen, we never fire first. Fire yourselves,' he replied dismissively, in perfect English. For a moment, it looked as though the battle might be postponed indefinitely, in a crazy ritual of 'After you – no, after you'. It is not certain who did actually fire first, although one account suggests, maybe unconvincingly, that the French loosed off a volley before the English had 'done laughing' at their sergeant's prayer for divine assistance. What is certain is that Lord Charles' guards subsequently fixed bayonets in a businesslike charge of the French lines which dislodged them from their position.

By the time the battle finished, at around two o' clock – just in time for a little late lunch for the aristocratic commanders – a total of some 15,000 soldiers had been killed. But whatever the precise truth of the story, the very fact it was so popular and repeated so often demonstrates what a gentlemanly business warfare was believed to be in the eighteenth century.

Facing the conquerors

King Christian X of Denmark was known for his habit of taking a morning ride without bodyguards through the streets of Copenhagen, during which his subjects were free to approach him.

These rides continued even after the Nazi occupation of the country, and the elderly King Christian mounted his own silent protest against the occupiers by publicly ignoring them. A long and fulsome telegram from Adolf Hitler congratulating him on his seventy-second birthday in 1942 received the dismissive reply: '*Meinen besten Dank, Chr. Rex*' ('My thanks, King Christian') – a slight that led to the recall of the German ambassador from Copenhagen and the expulsion of the Danish ambassador from Germany.

There were even stories that the king had responded to a German threat to force Danish Jews to wear a yellow star on their clothing by volunteering to wear one himself. There were no Danish Jews and gentiles in Copenhagen – only Danes.

Although the king's popularity angered senior German officers, they knew that any mistreatment of him might cause widespread trouble among the people.

In another well-documented incident, word was brought to King Christian that the swastika was flying over Christiansborg, the home of the Danish Rigsdag, or parliament. He immediately ordered that it should be taken down and replaced with the Danish flag.

This was done, but within hours, the German commandant had ordered that the swastika, the mark of German domination and Danish defeat, should be hoisted again on the palace flagpole.

King Christian telephoned him, and told him that if this were done, then a Danish soldier would be ordered to remove it again. In that case, said the commandant, the soldier would be shot by the German guards. 'I think not,' King Christian said. 'I will be that soldier.'

The swastika never flew above the Rigsdag.

Courteous, considerate & kind

The most dreadful of wars often start, at least, with a commitment to human decency, restraint and honourable behaviour. The horrific reality of trench warfare was still in the future when Lord Kitchener, Britain's Secretary of State for War, sent this message individually to each of the soldiers leaving for France in the British Expeditionary Force in August 1914: 'You are ordered abroad as a soldier of the king to help our French comrades against the invasion of a common enemy. You have to perform a task which will need your courage, your energy, your patience.' It said:

Remember that the honour of the British Army depends on your individual conduct. It will be your duty not only to set an example of discipline and perfect steadiness under fire but also to maintain the most friendly relations with those whom you are helping in this struggle. The operations in which you are engaged will, for the most part, take place in a friendly country, and you can do your own country no better service than in showing yourself in France and Belgium in the true character of a British soldier.

Be invariably courteous, considerate and kind. Never do anything likely to injure or destroy property, and always look upon looting as a disgraceful act. You are sure to meet a welcome and to be trusted; your conduct must justify that welcome and that trust.

Your duty cannot be done unless your health is sound. So keep constantly on your guard against any excesses. In this new experience you may find temptations both in wine and women. You must entirely resist both temptations, and, while treating all women with perfect courtesy, you should avoid any intimacy.

Do your duty bravely. Fear God. Honour the King.

Nearly ninety years later, in another war on another continent – almost in another world – Lieutenant Colonel Tim Collins used very different language to convey much the same message to around 800 men of the Royal Irish Regiment as they waited to cross the border in the allied invasion of Iraq in March 2003. Speaking off the cuff, without notes, he urged them to respect the Iraqi people:

We go to liberate, not to conquer. We will not fly our flags in their country. We are entering Iraq to free a people and the only flag which will be flown in that ancient land is their own. Show respect for them.

Don't treat them as refugees, for they are in their own country. Their children will be poor; in years to come they will know that the light of liberation in their lives was brought by you.

If there are casualties of war then remember that when they woke up and got dressed in the morning they did not plan to die this day. Allow them dignity in death. Bury them properly and mark their graves … If you harm the regiment or its history by over-enthusiasm in killing or in cowardice, know it is your family who will suffer. You will be shunned unless your conduct is of the highest – for your deeds will follow you down through history. We will bring shame on neither our uniform or our nation.

✧

Our sons as well

Among the thousands of tributes all over Britain to the dead of two world wars are one or two that stand out because they extend their grief to former enemies. At Wareham in Dorset, the bodies of German soldiers, sailors and airmen of the Second World War – some of them washed ashore and others those of prisoners from nearby prisoner-of-war camps – lie in graves that are mingled among those of the British dead.

And in a village churchyard in Suffolk can be found a memorial to the crew of a zeppelin airship that crashed nearby during the Second World War. A few minutes before the crash, the crew could have been dropping bombs on the people beneath – but after burying them, the villagers had the following passage from the Bible inscribed in their memory: 'Who art thou that judgest another man's servant? To his own master he standeth or falleth.'

But perhaps the most generous tribute of all came after the terrible fighting between Allied and Turkish troops for the Gallipoli Peninsula during the First World War in 1915–16, which cost the lives of hundreds of thousands of men on both sides. Many were buried where they fell, and after the Allied retreat there was great anguish among the families of those who had died over how their graves would be treated by the Turks – particularly because stories of the alleged barbaric actions of both German and Turkish troops were commonplace in wartime Britain.

In fact, the graves were treated with honour, and after the war the bodies were re-interred in either Turkish or Commonwealth War Commission cemeteries, which are still beautifully tended to this day.

Turkey's Prime Minister, Mustafa Kemal Atatürk, who had commanded a Turkish infantry division during the fighting for Gallipoli, caused a memorial to be erected on the peninsula, on which were inscribed words generously addressed to the mothers of the fallen Allied soldiers: 'You, the mothers who sent their sons from faraway countries, wipe away your tears. Your sons are now lying in our bosom, and are at peace. After having lost their lives on this land, they are our sons as well.'

Few former enemies can ever have paid such a chivalrous, dignified and moving tribute to those against whom they had once fought.

❧

A battle won

A good general never panics – and neither does a gentleman, as this story demonstrates. Lord Uxbridge led the charge of the heavy cavalry of the Royal Scots Greys at the Battle of Waterloo, taking more than 3,000 French prisoners. Later in the day, he was sitting on his horse next to the Duke of Wellington, watching the final stages of the battle, when a stray cannonball screamed through the air between them.

Uxbridge glanced down. 'By God, sir, I've lost my leg!' he exclaimed.

'By God, sir, so you have!' replied the duke.

The exchange was immortalised by Thomas Hardy in *The Dynasts*, his epic drama of the Napoleonic Wars. Hardy has Wellington, sitting astride his horse Copenhagen, going on to say:

Ay – the wind o' the shot
Blew past the withers of my Copenhagen
Like the foul sweeping of a witch's broom.
Aha! They are giving way!

The aristocratic insouciance which this story demonstrates, incidentally, did not mean that Wellington had no sense of the bloodshed and suffering that were the price of victory. In a sombre letter home after the battle, he observed sadly: 'My heart is broken by the terrible loss I have sustained in my old friends and companions and my poor soldiers. Believe me, nothing except a battle lost can be half so melancholy as a battle won.'

An affair of honour

For many years, the military authorities had an ambiguous attitude towards duelling. On the one hand, it exemplified the military virtues of courage and elan – but on the other, it was an extraordinarily wasteful way of getting rid of young officers.

As commander of the Allied armies in the peninsula and then in France during the Napoleonic Wars of 1803–15, the Duke of Wellington ordered that any of his officers who were involved in a duel would be severely punished. Nonetheless, in March 1829, by which time Wellington had become prime minister, he challenged another Tory politician, the Earl of Winchelsea, to a duel over a slight to his honour.

The quarrel had its origin in Wellington's promotion of Catholic emancipation. Winchelsea, who vigorously opposed improving the constitutional position of Roman

Catholics, wrote to several newspapers accusing Wellington of treachery. His honour impugned, and despite his views on duelling, Wellington called Winchelsea out. The duel took place on Battersea Fields, London (now Battersea Park), a popular site for these 'affairs of honour', on 21 March. At the word the two men, armed with pistols, moved apart, then turned and faced each other at a distance of twelve paces to fire their single shot. Wellington fired, and missed. Winchelsea then 'deloped', deliberately firing his weapon in the air rather than take advantage of his now defenceless adversary. Honour was satisfied and the quarrel declared over.

Wellington later claimed that he had fired at Winchelsea's legs, to wound rather than kill him; since he was a notoriously poor shot, however, and was just as likely to have hit a vital spot, the other man was probably luckier than he knew. King's College, University of London, founded in 1829 by non-Anglican Christians and followers of other faiths, still celebrates 'Duel Day' on 21 March each year.

It has to be said that Winchelsea's graceful act in sparing the Great Duke when he had him at his mercy was perhaps at least as wise as it was selfless. Duelling was in any case illegal by that time, and to have killed or wounded the man who was not only prime minister, but also the greatest commander in British history and a popular hero as well, could easily have led to the earl being torn to pieces by a mob.

In fact, the whole custom of duelling has always been hedged around with courtesies and formalities, which have occasionally been used by those who have more shrewdness than courage to avoid a fight that they seemed likely to lose.

A century before Wellington, Sir William Petty, who served under Oliver Cromwell as a surveyor in Ireland, was challenged to a duel because of some real or imagined slight. Sir William was a man of many talents – doctor, mathematician, statistician and political economist – but he was not a fighter, and since his challenger was an officer with long and bloody experience in Cromwell's army, it seemed likely that he would come off second best. Worse, Petty was known to be extremely short-sighted.

However, since he was the one being challenged, he was entitled to choose where the duel was to be fought and what weapons should be used. For the place, he chose a pitch-dark cellar, and the weapons, carpenter's axes. His ingenuity brought the whole challenge into public ridicule, and so the duel – doubtless to Sir William's considerable relief – was cancelled.

A noble gesture made in vain

In March 1199, as he laid siege to the French town of Chalus, the great Richard Coeur de Lion – Richard the Lionheart – was wounded by a crossbow bolt shot from the walls by a young townsman. He went to his tent to try to pull it out, but eventually had to call in a surgeon who, according to the ancient chroniclers, made such a mess of the job that the wound became infected and gangrenous. By the time the town fell, the king was close to death.

He ordered that the young man who had shot him – named Bertrand de Gourdon in some of the chronicles – should be brought before him. 'What harm have I ever done you, that you should want to kill me?' he asked.

Bertrand, apparently unafraid of the king, his soldiers or the terrible punishments that probably lay in store for him, answered defiantly that his father and two of his brothers had been killed by Richard. 'Do what you will,' he said. 'I will die happy, if I can be sure that I have ridded the world of a tyrant who has defiled it with blood and slaughter' – not the most tactful speech for a man in his position, perhaps, but Richard was impressed with his spirit. He ordered that he should be set free, and gave him a hundred marks to help him on his way. It was a final noble gesture of chivalry by a king who was more often feared for his brutality in the field than praised for his magnanimity.

As a sad little footnote to this story of royal restraint and generosity, however, it is worth reporting that King Richard's gesture did Bertrand little good. As soon as the king was dead his military commander, the Provencal mercenary Mercadier seized the money for himself and had the young man flayed alive.

❧

A chivalrous commander

The classical chroniclers Livy and Plutarch tell the story of a schoolteacher in the Etruscan town of Falerii in 394 BC, which was being besieged by the Roman dictator Camillus. He used to take the young boys in his care – the sons of some of the town's leading citizens – for walks outside the town walls. Day by day he took them a little further from the town, persuading them each time that there was nothing to fear, until eventually he led them in among the outposts of Camillus' army and demanded to be taken to the Roman leader.

Hoping to win the general's favour, and a large reward, the schoolteacher declared that he had brought the boys to him so that the city would surrender.

Camillus, however, was shocked. 'Even war has laws which good and brave men will respect,' he said. 'We must not pursue victory so ardently that we do not recoil from the gifts of shameful and ungodly men. I am a great general who will rely on my own courage to wage war, not on the baseness of other people.'

Then, showing that he had a sense of humour to match his sense of honour, he ordered that the schoolmaster should be stripped naked, and the boys be given whips and sticks so that they might drive him back into the city.

Sometimes, even in battle, virtue can be its own reward. The people of Falerii were so impressed by a general who valued justice more highly than conquest that they surrendered. The chroniclers don't say what they did with the schoolmaster.

Sauce for the goose

Restraint is not the most notable military virtue – few fights are won by pulling punches. But just sometimes, a military commander can enjoy the great satisfaction of holding back and allowing his enemy to dig a hole for himself.

The story is told of the exchange between the German and French delegations as negotiations got under way for the Armistice of 1919. The commander of the French forces, Marshal Foch, read out a list of conditions. The Germans were appalled. 'These are terms upon which no civilised nation could insist,' exclaimed one of the German generals.

'They are indeed,' replied Foch quietly and courteously. 'These are not the French terms today. These are the terms which the German commander imposed on the city of Lille when it surrendered.'

The wreck of the *Birkenhead*

HMS *Birkenhead* was an iron-hulled 210ft paddle steamer which was used as a troopship by the Royal Navy in the mid-nineteenth century. In February 1852 she made a brief refuelling stop at Simonstown in South Africa, after the long trip from Cork. On board were 132 ship's officers and crew, and some 480 soldiers from several different regiments, bound for the Frontier War that was being waged against Xhosa tribesmen in the Eastern Cape. With them were twenty women and children and several cavalry horses.

Early in the morning of 26 February, about half a mile off the ominously named Danger Point, near Cape Town, the ship struck a submerged rock and started to sink almost at once. Scores of men were drowned in their bunks – and when the crew tried to launch the lifeboats, they discovered that only three were serviceable. The bolts securing the rest were immoveable with rust and paint.

As the sailors struggled to free the boats, the soldiers stood in line on the tossing deck, awaiting orders as if they were on the parade ground. Some manned the pumps, some threw the horses overboard to try and swim for the shore, and others joined the fruitless struggle to launch more boats.

The rest – many of them little more than boys who had been in the army for only a few months – stood silently in their ranks, as though waiting for an inspection. Soon after the women and children had been helped into the boats and rowed away, the ship began to break up.

At this point, the *Birkenhead*'s captain shouted that all the men who could swim should try to make for the boats, but Lieutenant-Colonel Alexander Seton of the 74th Highlanders, the soldiers' commanding officer, realised that there was the danger that the boats would be swamped if they did so. He gave the order to stand firm, and the women and children watched as the soldiers, still without panicking or losing their discipline, were thrown into the sea as the ship sank in less than twenty minutes. Those who could swim tried to make for the shore, but few of them made it. Almost all were accounted for by cold and exhaustion, by the heavy seas, which pounded them against the rocks, and by the Great White sharks – later named Tommy Sharks after the soldiers or 'Tommies' who died.

Over 430 soldiers and sailors died in the shipwreck, including Lieutenant-Colonel Seton and the ship's captain, Robert Salmond; only 193 were saved. But among them were all the women and children; the discipline, courage and chivalry of the men on board, accepting almost certain death to give their loved ones the chance of survival, had not been in vain.

At the time of the *Birkenhead* disaster, the Royal Navy had no pre-planned emergency drill; it was the example of that day that led to the cry of 'Women and children first', the so-called '*Birkenhead* drill', which became the tradition in abandoning ship. Rudyard Kipling's poem *Soldier an' Sailor Too*, written more than forty years later, captured the lasting popular emotion about the *Birkenhead* story with his line: 'To stand an' be still to the *Birken'ead* drill, is a damn' tough bullet to chew.'

But perhaps the best tribute came in the direct, unemotional words of one of the survivors to the court martial that followed the disaster:

The order and regularity that prevailed on board, from the moment the ship struck till she totally disappeared, far exceeded anything that I had thought could be affected by the best discipline; and it is the more to be wondered at seeing that most of the soldiers were but a short time in the service.

The remains of the *Birkenhead* still lie in about thirty metres of water, where she sank – a hidden, silent, but intensely evocative memorial to a story of true heroism and military discipline.

Hero or villain?

Andy McNab, the best-selling author and former member of the Special Air Services, says that soldiers – special forces soldiers, at least – never talk about 'the enemy'. Instead, they use the neutral term 'players'.

It's an acceptance that, in most conflicts, both sides are doing much the same thing: if the soldiers on one side had happened to be born somewhere else, then they might have been fighting in a different army. They may have more in common with the men they are fighting than modern politicians, and maybe even senior officers, might like to admit.

It's a professional attitude towards war that avoids blowing bugles and waving flags, and it's one that has been prevalent for centuries, not just with soldiers but sometimes with the kings who used to command them as well.

An eighteenth century collection of anecdotes, the *Pocket Remembrancer* of 1775, tells the story of a French king taken to see the monument at Rouen to the memory of

England's Duke of Bedford. The French have no reason to remember the fifteenth century duke with any affection; as regent for the young Henry VI he rampaged through their countryside, defeated their armies, raped and pillaged in their towns and villages, and finally had their national hero, Joan of Arc, burned at the stake.

Bearing all this in mind, suggested one of the courtiers of the French king as he gazed on the monument, it might be a good idea to have the whole thing torn stone from stone to try to forget about a particularly painful period of French history.

The king – sadly the *Pocket Remembrancer* does not say which king it was – pondered for a moment. 'By no means,' he said finally. 'Let us not dare to disturb the ashes of a man who when he was living made all France tremble.'

Within a few years of the *Pocket Remembrancer*'s publication, of course, the French Revolution had swept away much more than just a monument to a long-dead foreign warrior. Today only a modern inscription in Rouen Cathedral notes that the Duke of Bedford ever existed at all – but the story of the respect and generosity of an unknown French king still remains. Andy McNab would probably approve.

A gesture of loyalty

In 334 BC, Alexander the Great was about to embark on the invasion of Asia which would lead to the destruction of the

Persian Empire and spread Greek civilisation as far as the foothills of the Himalayas.

He was determined that his generals should be able to leave their families well provided for while they campaigned with him – partly, no doubt, so that he could be sure of their loyalty and continuing commitment to his cause – and so he made grants to each of them of estates, villages and other property that would provide an income while they were away.

When he had nearly completed this distribution of most of the lands he possessed in Macedonia, his friend and loyal general Perdiccas asked whether he was keeping anything back for himself. 'I have my hopes,' said Alexander.

'Then we, your companions, will share in your hopes,' replied Perdiccas, refusing the land that Alexander was offering him. Several other generals did the same, preferring to show their loyalty to Alexander and his whole enterprise than to take possession of his lands before they had even set off.

∽

A 'verray parfit, gentil knighte'

The Elizabethans valued courtesy as highly as courage – and knew that the two were often closely related.

Sir Philip Sidney, poet, courtier and soldier, was held to be the model of knightly virtue – the epitome of what Chaucer referred to as 'a verray parfit, gentil knighte' – and his death at the age of 31, fighting against the Spanish at the Battle of Zutphen in the Netherlands, September 1586, was greeted with shock in Queen Elizabeth's court. Sir Philip had been wounded in the thigh, and died after nearly a month in agony as the wound became poisoned.

But the story of his heroism was told almost immediately: lying injured and in great pain on the battlefield, he had handed his water bottle to an ordinary soldier who was close to death, with the words, 'Thy necessity is yet greater than mine.' For the Elizabethans, and for every age since, it was the sort of behaviour that meant that his name would live forever – and more than 400 years later, his statue still stands in Zutphen, close to where he fell.

I'M A CELEBRITY, GET ME OUT OF HERE - PLEASE!

It may be hard to feel sorry for celebrities and 'personalities'. The glitzy characters who habitually pop up on television, on anything from *Big Brother* or *I'm a Celebrity* to the TV news, often don't make it easy for people to like them off screen. Television breeds self-importance, and self-importance is the enemy of courtesy.

Sometimes, bad behaviour can bring its own reward: there is a famous sequence of photographs that show a young Mick Jagger leaving a nightclub. In the first, he has just angrily spotted the photographer; the second shows him waving an angry finger in the photographer's direction, and in the third, he is striding purposefully towards him, apparently intent on inflicting punishment. In the fourth, he is stretched embarrassingly on his back in the road, clearly having come off second best.

But to be fair, celebrities from A-list to D-list often have a lot to put up with: constantly flashing cameras, occasionally rude and unwelcome questions, and all the pressures of life in the spotlight. And yet some of them manage, with random acts of courtesy, grace and dignity, to demonstrate that they have personalities that go beyond just being a personality.

Can I have your autograph?

A personal story to begin with. As a young boy in the 1960s, I was at Headingley for a cricket test match, and I had been diligently filling in a scorebook all day, as young boys do. Every detail of the play was there, spelled out in dots, lines, figures, names and w's to mark the wickets for anyone who could read it. Looking up from my labours, I saw the actor James Ellis – a star of one of my favourite television programmes, a police series called *Z Cars* – standing nearby watching the match.

Since *Z Cars* was even more of a passion than cricket, I went nervously up to him hoping for an autograph – but since I had, even at that young age, a modicum of street wisdom I didn't ask him straight away. Instead, reasoning that he probably hadn't been there for long, I held out my book towards him. 'Would you like to see the scorebook?' I asked, shyly.

He seemed pleased, and spent several minutes looking over what had happened. Eventually, when he handed back the book with a thank you and a smile, I guessed it was the right time. 'Could I have your autograph?' I asked.

'Come back at the end of play and you can. If I sign it for you now, I'll have to sign dozens of them,' he said. Slightly crestfallen, I took my book and went back to my seat and my scoring. Then, when play finished for the day, I went back hopefully to where I had left him – to find that he had gone. I couldn't believe it; after all, he'd *promised*. I told myself I understood why he didn't want to be pestered by autograph hunters, and why he'd slipped away – but I didn't. It was the first time I'd actually been told a direct lie by a grown up, and it hurt.

And then, a few days later, I was leafing idly through my scorebook – and there, on the next blank page, were those magic words: 'James Ellis, PC Lynch, Z Cars.' He must have scribbled them in while I wasn't looking – taking a chance on being spotted by any of the other small boys hanging around. He didn't need to do it, and he never knew how much it meant to a 12-year-old boy. But it wasn't a bad example of courtesy and thoughtfulness, and I've never forgotten it.

Would you care to sit down? And you? And you?

The essayist, novelist and poet G.K. Chesterton wrote well over a hundred books during a thirty-six year literary career.

As he grew older, his wit, his bumptious enthusiasm and his recognisability – he was an extremely fat man, with a pince-nez and a bristling moustache – made him a celebrity before the age of television.

His wit could be biting, and he neither asked nor gave quarter in any of his literary, social or theological quarrels – but he was passionate about courtesy, and had a lively sense of humour about himself, particularly about his large size. At one lecture in the 1930s he told his audience: 'Just the other day in the Underground, I enjoyed the pleasure of offering my seat to three ladies.'

Don't die of embarrassment

Some subjects are not mentioned in polite conversation, and some words are never used. This convention may avoid embarrassment, but it can also lead to confusion, and even to tragedy.

One story, told by the famous raconteur and wit Ned Sherrin in his book *In His Anecdotage*, is an example of the misunderstandings that can arise from excessive propriety. Queen Mary, the former Princess of Teck in the Kingdom of Württemberg, and wife of King George V, was a kindly and considerate woman, but she was known for her awesome regal formality and propriety. On one occasion, she noticed that her senior detective had been missing for several days, and asked an equerry whether he was sick.

In fact, the policeman was at home, enduring a severe case of piles. Uncomfortable, embarrassing and making it difficult to sit down, perhaps, but hardly life-threatening. Yet the equerry felt he could not pass such intimate and indelicate information on to Her Majesty, and simply mumbled that the detective was suffering from 'an unfortunate disease'. The queen, no doubt grateful for his discretion, nodded sympathetically and said nothing.

A few days later, King George spoke to a second palace official. 'What are we going to do about this detective?' he asked.

'Oh sir, he'll be back soon,' came the reply. 'He's only got an attack of piles.'

The king, relieved but slightly puzzled, paused for a moment. 'Some fool of an equerry told my wife he had syphilis,' he said.

But often, the consequences can be much more serious. Elizabeth Branwell, the maiden aunt of the Brontë sisters who helped their widowed father with their upbringing in the Yorkshire village of Haworth, died of exhaustion brought on by constipation. A Victorian gentlewoman of high morality and considerable sternness, who would have approved unreservedly of the equerry's reticence, she was far too well brought-up to tell the doctor what her trouble might be.

Doctors still occasionally struggle against such evasiveness. One friend of the author's, being treated for cancer, was urged by his consultant not to hesitate to ask any question or report any symptom, however awkward it may be to find the words.

'You may die from cancer, although we'll do all that we possibly can to see that you don't,' the doctor said. 'But it would be a great waste to die of embarrassment.'

He didn't, incidentally, thanks to the NHS, and survives to tell the story.

Health & safety

The BBC's human resources department is known throughout the corporation for its occasionally pernickety attitude towards health and safety. Cameramen who may one week be dodging bullets in Afghanistan sometimes complain that a few days later they may have to listen to official instructions about how to climb a ladder.

In 2007, the BBC correspondent Damien Grammaticus was sent to report on the disastrous floods in Bangladesh which killed hundreds of people and left millions more homeless. This unavoidably involved travelling around the flooded villages in the motorboats that were being used to rescue stranded villagers.

There were several complaints to the BBC that Grammaticus and his team were taking up spaces that could have been used by refugees – an issue that concerned the correspondent himself as well – but the decision was taken that it was important that the story and the pictures should reach the world at large. By taking the video footage and reporting on the disaster, the team could help to encourage international aid that would help even more victims of the floods.

Back in London, however, HR staff had noticed something else: Grammaticus had been seen on screen reporting from a moving boat without wearing a lifejacket. This was potentially a serious 'health and safety' offence, and questions were asked of his newsroom bosses.

It turned out that the BBC correspondent and his team had insisted that their safety equipment should be used by some of the refugees who were piled into their boats. He has never spoken publicly about this, and can't understand why anyone would be interested in the story.

Getting the message across

Many people believe they have better manners than they actually have – only a very few make the opposite mistake. The writer Evelyn Waugh, however, author of such well-loved classics as *Scoop* and *Brideshead Revisited*, was taken aback by a letter from his friend, the society beauty Lady Diana Cooper. In it, she said that her husband Duff Cooper had been surprised and grieved by a report he had heard that Waugh had detested him for more than twenty years.

'I am very sorry to hear that,' Waugh replied. 'I must have nicer manners than people normally credit me with.'

Or maybe not; one of Waugh's other remarks on the subject ought to be noted as well. 'Manners,' he once said, 'are especially the need of the plain. The pretty can get away with anything.'

A backhanded blessing

Sir William Davenant was a famous and highly respected poet and dramatist of the seventeenth century, who is now buried in Poet's Corner in Westminster Abbey. Apart from his literary efforts, his celebrity in his own day derived partly from his encouragement of the rumour that he was the illegitimate son of William Shakespeare – a rumour which, the gossip John Aubrey cruelly pointed out, gave his mother 'a very light report, whereby she was called a whore'.

Aubrey also recounts how he caught either gonorrhoea or syphilis from 'a black handsome wench that he lay in Axe Yard, Westminster', and, as a result, lost his nose.

Sir William was constantly being offended by the cruel jokes and ribaldry that his misfortune caused among the wits of literary London, so he was deeply touched by the courtesy of a simple old woman who saw him in the street, commented on his condition, and offered him her blessings on his eyesight.

'Why would you bless my eyes, woman?' he asked.

She explained that without a nose, should his eyesight begin to fail, there would be nowhere to balance a pair of spectacles.

Business tactics

The nineteenth-century French novelist Alexandre Dumas, *père*, author of *The Three Musketeers* and *The Count of Monte Cristo*, won fame first as a brilliantly successful playwright whose works could be guaranteed to fill any theatre in Paris.

One day, he was visited by the angry manager of one of the biggest theatres in the city, who stormed into Dumas' room in his hat and coat, and demanded to know if the rumour was true that Dumas' latest play had been sold to a smaller rival.

Indeed it was, said Dumas, and the theatre manager immediately made a huge bid of his own in return. It was much bigger than the other company's offer, and the manager had no doubt that Dumas would accept it without demur.

But the famous playwright shook his head. He would stand by the bargain he had made, he said, particularly because of the tactic that the representative of the smaller company had used to persuade him to sign the contract.

'And what was that?' the disappointed bidder asked.

Simple, said Dumas; 'When he spoke to me, he removed his hat.'

❧

Death on the *Titanic*

Many myths and legends have gathered around the sinking of the *Titanic* in April 1912 – but one of the best authenticated is that of the courage and chivalry of Benjamin Guggenheim, the fabulously wealthy fifth son of the legendary mining magnate Meyer Guggenheim, and one of the biggest celebrities of his day.

The 46-year-old Benjamin had boarded the ship at Southampton for her maiden transatlantic voyage, along with his mistress, a French singer named Léontine Aubart, her maid Emma Sägesser, Guggenheim's valet Victor Giglio (with whom he shared a stateroom) and his chauffeur René Pernot.

After the liner struck an iceberg shortly before midnight on Sunday 14 April, Guggenheim and Giglio helped the two women into one of the lifeboats. It was nothing, Guggenheim reassured them in German, the ship only required a repair and would soon resume its voyage: 'We will soon see each other again!'

But it was clear by then that his optimism was ill-founded; with the lifeboat launched, he and Giglio returned to their stateroom, took off the lifejackets and heavy sweaters they had been wearing, and donned full evening dress. 'We have dressed in our best, and are prepared to go down like gentlemen,' one survivor remembered hearing him say. Another was given a message for Guggenheim's wife in New York. 'If anything should happen to me, tell her I've done my best in doing my duty,' he said.

Both he and Giglio perished, as did the chauffeur, whose second class cabin was in a different part of the ship. Léontine Aubart and Emma Sägesser survived to be rescued, however, and lived on into the 1960s, both dying in their late seventies.

❧

A circumspect reply

Often, particularly when dealing with a vain and ageing film star, courtesy may amount to little more than intelligent self-interest. Who wants to upset a good client, when all you have to do to keep her sweet is swallow an obvious reply? You can, after all, tell the truth and still be courteous – and circumspect. Take this reported exchange between Marlene Dietrich and an anonymous photographer.

'Your photographs are not so good any more,' she told him. 'Eight years ago, you used to make me look wonderful.'

'Yes,' he replied, nodding sadly. 'But I was much younger then.'

Superstar

Modern performers sometimes seem to equate star quality with rudeness – but the late Sammy Davis Junior showed that it can often be something very similar to courtesy. Back in the 1960s, he was performing at a club in Lake Tahoe, Nevada, before a crowd of some 800 diners.

He opened with three of his old favourites, but well before he had reached the end of the third song, it was clear that he wasn't on top form. He stopped, thought for a moment, and then picked up the microphone again. 'Folks, some nights I can do it, and some nights I can't. I guess tonight, I can't,' he said, shaking his head regretfully. 'I'm really sorry to let you down, but I guess the least I can do is ask you all to be my guests.'

With that, he left the club – having first paid more than $17,000 for the food and drinks of the entire audience.

A modest composer

The German Romantic composer Johannes Brahms enjoyed a period of staggering popularity in the late nineteenth century, lionised across Europe both for his original compositions and for his skill as a conductor. However, this adulation could not turn his head, and he remained a modest man who hated flattery. Two stories make the point.

He was invited to dinner by one of the greatest wine connoisseurs of Hamburg, his home town, and as the first bottle was poured, the host explained that it was the finest wine in his extensive cellar. 'This,' he told the assembled company, 'is the Johannes Brahms of my collection.'

As he watched anxiously, Brahms picked up his glass, swirled the wine around the bowl, and inhaled its delicate bouquet. Finally, he took a sip, and then put the glass down again without comment. After a moment or two, his anxious host could wait no more. 'How do you like it?' he asked nervously.

'Delicious, truly delicious, my friend,' replied Brahms. 'But I think I would like to try your Beethoven.'

On another occasion, in November 1881, Brahms attended an official dinner in the Hungarian capital, Budapest, after performing as soloist in the first performance of his own *Second Piano Concerto*. The work, which Brahms himself described as 'the long terror', is a challenge for any pianist, but is widely considered one of his most impressive compositions.

At the dinner, as the guests were being invited to drink a toast to 'Germany's most celebrated composer,' Brahms interrupted. 'Quite right – Gentlemen, here's to Mozart!' he said.

In fact, there was another finely judged expression of courtesy after Brahms performed the same piece sometime later, this time from one of the critics. There was no doubting the originality and power of the composition, but Brahms' own playing was little more than competent. The critic

Eduard Hanslick, a close friend of the composer and a fervent admirer of his work, wrote that Brahms now had more important things to do than to practise for hours each day.

After all, who would be the person to tell Johannes Brahms that his playing was not up to scratch?

An undeserved rebuff

Courtesy, of course, is not always repaid in kind. The American poet and anthologist Louis Untermeyer was once invited to speak to a small literary group, and accepted their offer of a fee for his efforts. When he attended their meeting, however, he saw for himself how limited their resources were, and generously returned the money to their treasurer, saying that he was sure that it could be put to a good use.

Meeting the man again sometime later, he inquired what 'good use' they had found for it. Slightly incautiously, the treasurer replied that it had been paid into a fund to get better speakers to address their meetings.

A most famous greeting

Few people have heard of John Rowlands, who was born into a poor Welsh family, grew up in the workhouse, and emigrated to the United States at the age of 18 to seek his fortune. There he was taken in by a wealthy merchant who gave him a job, a home and a new name, Henry Morton Stanley. The young man eventually forged a career for himself as a journalist, and was subsequently sent by the *New York Herald* to find out what had happened to the famous British explorer, Dr David Livingstone.

His book *How I Found Livingstone*, written some years later, describes the moment of his success in Ujiji, near Lake Tanganyika in present-day Tanzania. There in the jungle, the two men addressed each other with the stilted, slightly awkward courtesy of Victorian gentlemen, and Stanley uttered what has become probably the most famous greeting of all time:

As I advanced slowly towards him, I noticed he was pale, looked wearied, had a grey beard, wore a bluish cap with a faded gold band round it, had on a red-sleeved waistcoat and a pair of grey tweed trousers. I would have run to him, only I was a coward in the presence of such a mob, would have embraced him, only, he being an Englishman, I did not know how he would receive me. So I did what cowardice and false pride suggested was the best thing – walked deliberately up to him, took off my hat, and said, 'Dr. Livingstone, I presume?'

'Yes,' said he, with a kind smile, lifting his cap slightly.

I replace my hat on my head and he puts on his cap, and we both grasp hands, and I then say aloud, 'I thank God, Doctor, I have been permitted to see you'.

He answered, 'I feel thankful that I am here to welcome you'.

❧

Generosity & sensitivity

By 1873 the French landscape painter Jean-Baptiste-Camille Corot enjoyed a glittering reputation among the connoisseurs and art dealers of Paris. His canvases sold for thousands of francs, and he was a wealthy man, known for the generosity of his donations to charities. He could also show remarkable sensitivity towards the feelings of those he tried to help.

He heard that the caricaturist, painter and sculptor Honoré Daumier, whose work he had admired for many years, was nearly blind, living in poverty and threatened with eviction from his cottage in the village of Valmondois because he could not afford to pay the rent.

Corot secretly bought him a house, and wrote to explain what he had done:

My old friend ... I have a little house at Valmondois for which I cannot think of a use. It occurred to me that I could give it to you, and since I like the idea, I have already registered it in your name. I'm not trying to do you a good turn – simply trying to annoy your landlord.

Daumier's reply was brief but heartfelt: 'You are the only man from whom I could accept such a gift without humiliation.' Afterwards, the two artists painted each other's portraits in the garden of Daumier's new home, and it was from there that he travelled to attend the first solo exhibition of his life, just a year before he died. Corot's generous and sensitive gesture had given him a few years of peace and simple comfort after a lifetime of struggle.

❧

Correcting a mistake

It's not only conventionally nice people who are capable of sudden and instinctive acts of kindness, generosity and courtesy. The legendary motor magnate Henry Ford, for example, was known to be a ruthless bully in his private life, an anti-union despot in his factories and an early anti-Semitic supporter of Adolf Hitler – maybe not the first man you would turn to for charitable contributions.

But on a visit to Dublin – Ford was proud of his Irish roots, and tried to buy his ancestral home at Ballinascarty – he donated £2,000 towards the construction of a new orphanage. His gesture was spread all over the front of the next day's papers, but a careless reporter or an incompetent typesetter reported his gift as £20,000. Embarrassed, the director of the appeal went to Ford's hotel to apologise, and said he would phone the newspaper editor at once to insist that the mistake should be corrected.

'No need,' said Ford. 'Why don't I just give you the remaining £18,000 instead?' And he took out his cheque book at once and did just that.

A surprising donation

During the 1930s the Catholic Worker Movement ran a hostel for down-and-outs in New York. For many of them, it was their only refuge from life on the streets – but because it failed to meet the city's regulations, the organisation's founder, Dorothy Day, was fined $250.

On her way to pay the fine at New York's Manhattan Upper Court, she came upon a group of drunks and beggars gathered on a street corner, who were asking passers-by for money. She had almost passed them when one individual, indistinguishable from the rest, sidled forward and pressed a piece of paper into her hand. 'I read about your problems, lady, and I wanted to help. Here's two-fifty,' he mumbled, before drifting back into the crowd.

She thanked him as he disappeared: $2.50 would not go far towards paying the fine, but she was touched and delighted at this small gesture of support from what she assumed must have been one of the occupants of the hostel.

It was not until she had almost reached the court that she looked at what she had been given. It was not, as she had thought, a couple of banknotes, but a cheque. It was for $250, the full amount of her fine. And it was signed W.H. Auden.

She was sorry she hadn't recognised him, but it was understandable, as she said later, 'Poets do look a bit *unpressed*, don't they?'

Yet another rejection slip

Anyone who starts writing for a living knows what a rejection slip looks – and feels – like. By the time they've achieved success they've often forgotten. But a journalist who used to work with George Orwell on *Tribune* in the 1940s tells the story of how he found him, then the magazine's literary editor, stuffing something into a packet with a guilty look on his face.

One of the tasks which Orwell most disliked was sending back unaccepted submissions to their unlucky authors – and on this occasion, folding up the unusable verses that had been sent in along with the bland rejection slip, he was surreptitiously adding a 10s note of his own to the bundle. It was a small gesture, but it says much about Orwell and his feelings for the poor.

A strange invitation

There are many stories about William Archibald Spooner, Warden of New College, Oxford – most of them apocryphal. His famous inability to get his words right – telling an undergraduate he had 'tasted a whole worm', for instance, rather than 'wasted a whole term', and looking for a pub called the Dull Man in Greenwich when he should have been in the Green Man in Dulwich – brought the word Spoonerism into the language.

But for all his occasional confusion – especially in his old age when he was warden, or head, of his college – he was a kindly and courteous gentleman. In his seventies, he was walking in the college quadrangle when he met a stranger about whom he could remember nothing except that he was a newly appointed Fellow.

'I'd like you to come to tea tomorrow,' he beamed. 'I'm giving a little party in my room for the new Mathematics Fellow.'

The stranger, a much younger man, looked slightly embarrassed and very anxious not to cause offence. 'But Warden,' he stammered, 'I *am* the new Mathematics Fellow.'

Spooner was not remotely put off his stride. 'Never mind,' he said. 'Come all the same.' And off he went.

❧

A gentle awakening

The great Austrian classical pianist Artur Schnabel was known for his intellectual seriousness rather than his sense of humour; except for when he noticed one evening that an elderly woman in the front row of the audience at one of his recitals had fallen asleep.

As the audience applauded enthusiastically at the end of his performance, she suddenly jerked awake, and looked around guiltily. As the applause died away, Schnabel leant across to apologise. 'I'm sorry, madam, it was the clapping,' he said. 'I was playing as quietly as I can.'

ꙮ

The importance of a tie

Great artists and other celebrities may sometimes get away with ignoring the dress code that is suggested by their hosts – struggling up-and-coming writers, as the young Mark Twain found out, cannot.

Twain, his great novels still unwritten, was invited to the home of his neighbour, Mrs Harriet Beecher Stowe, in Hartford, Connecticut. Her anti-slavery novel, *Uncle Tom's Cabin*, had made her famous on both sides of the Atlantic, and she insisted on a proper deference. So when her guest, a genial and friendly man who often had little time for social formalities, turned up with his shirt collar undone, he was roundly upbraided by his hostess in front of all the other guests for not wearing a tie.

The next morning, a messenger arrived at the Stowes' front door, carrying a small parcel wrapped in brown paper. Inside was a black tie, and a note, which said: 'Here is a necktie. Please take it out and look at it. I believe I was with you for about half an hour without this necktie. At the end of that time, would you be good enough to return it, as it is the only one I have. Mark Twain.'

～❧～

Jesse James or Robin Hood?

The American outlaw Jesse James terrorised the American West in the aftermath of the Civil War, shooting and killing bank employees and anyone else who got in his way, while at the same time assiduously burnishing his image as a Robin Hood figure who stole from the rich to give to the poor.

While he certainly earned the first part of that reputation, there is little evidence that he ever did much giving, either to the poor or anyone else. But scores of stories grew up about him, many of them describing his courtesy and elan.

One tells of an elderly widow at whose house the James gang stayed while they were on the run from the law. She had no idea that they were outlaws, and opened her heart to them, describing her struggle against poverty since the death of her husband and telling them how hard she was finding it to manage. The very next day, she said, a debt collector was coming to collect $1,400 which she owed to the bank – and since she had no money to give him, she would be evicted from her farm.

As the gang left the next morning, James handed her a packet. Inside was $1,400 with which she could pay off her debt – the proceeds, although she didn't know it, of Jesse James' latest raid. Brushing aside her thanks, the outlaw reminded her to demand a proper receipt for the money, and rode off with his companions.

After a short distance, they stopped in a clump of trees close to the trail and watched the debt collector ride past on his way to the farm. Then a few minutes later, as he rode back down the trail to take the money he had collected back to the bank, they held him up at gunpoint and took back the $1,400.

They had the money and the widow had her receipt, so everyone – or almost everyone – was happy.

One word of praise

The great actor Henry Compton – said to be the finest performer of Shakespeare's comic roles in the nineteenth century – was once buttonholed by an aspiring colleague who unwisely asked him: 'Do you think my performance last night was good?'

Unfortunately it hadn't been, but Compton didn't want to hurt his feelings. 'Good?' he asked enthusiastically. '*Good*, my dear chap? Good isn't the word …'

3

HOME IS WHERE ...

With our own families and in the privacy of our own homes, surely, we can act as we please. Many people, once they have closed the front door behind them, behave in ways that would make them ashamed in public. Home, perhaps, is where you hang your head – or at least, where you would if you thought for a moment about your behaviour.

But there's no reason why we should treat friends, work colleagues, and even complete strangers with courtesy and consideration, and then forget about the people closest to us. The stories in this chapter show how people have dealt with some of the problems we all face occasionally at home and in our daily lives. Sometimes they've got it wrong; sometimes they've ended up looking foolish – but they've generally had the very best of intentions.

A twinkle in his eye

It can sometimes be difficult to separate courtesy from affection. Maybe, in fact, the gentle demonstration of feeling is the truest courtesy between two people who are very close.

The Arabian traveller, poet and writer Charles Doughty, the author of the classic *Travels in Arabia Deserta*, could behave like a cantankerous old man even in his thirties – at the age of 35 he would point to his long beard and demand the respect to which he said he believed his great age entitled him. As he grew older he was not one to forget a slight or lay aside a grudge and he would bury himself in his books for days at a time, leaving his wife Caroline and their two daughters to look after themselves.

And yet, after forty years of marriage, he still treated Caroline with courtesy, affection and respect. Towards the end of his life, he would search out some newly budding flower in the garden and bring it inside for her, hiding it behind his back with a twinkle in his eye, and make her guess what it was that he had found.

He never realised, his daughters said later, that Caroline, who did all the gardening, had watched as all the flowers grew, and knew better than he did what was in bloom. So as he was doing his best to treat her with kindness by showing his affection with these spur-of-the-moment little gifts, she was returning the compliment by playing along with the game and pretending to be surprised.

Different recipes for a happy marriage

English people have traditionally been uneasy with public displays of affection: showing too much emotion towards one person, it seems, might be considered discourteous towards everyone else. In William Congreve's comedy *The Way of the World*, written in 1700, Millament sums up how she thinks a marriage should be conducted:

> Don't let us be familiar or fond, nor kiss before folks, like my Lady Fadler and Sir Francis ... Let us never visit together, nor go to a play together, but let us be very strange and well-bred. Let us be as strange as if we had been married a great while, and as well-bred as if we were not married at all.

Hardly a great recipe for a happy married life, then. And yet there are plenty of examples of people who have managed to remain impeccably well-bred, and still demonstrated their feelings quite openly. Being considerate towards the rest of the world, in other words, doesn't mean you have to be dismissive about the person you love.

For example, in the early 1940s the celebrated writer and caricaturist Sir Max Beerbohm, then in his seventies, was with his elderly wife at a party. A gaggle of young actresses and models were trying to catch his eye, all of them, as one guest said, 'painted ... with the determination to gain attention'. It must have been a flattering experience for the old man. But Beerbohm looked at them and shuddered, then turned to his wife and said, 'My dear, you are looking so charming tonight that I simply must talk to you.'

I believe in you

It's not just the relationships between lovers or husbands and wives that call for honesty, openness and consideration. The football manager David Jones appeared in court in December 2000, then in charge at the Premiership club Southampton, charged with the sexual abuse of young boys at a special school where he had once worked. The charges were later dismissed out of hand, with the judge telling him: 'No wrongdoing whatsoever on your part has been established.' But on that morning, Jones – married for twenty-three years and the father of four children – was facing the destruction of his entire world.

Then his 16-year-old daughter, Chloe, handed him a card:

Dad,

I never say this to your face, so I'm telling you on paper how much I love you. I'm not the world's most perfect child and I'm at an age where I never show affection towards my parents, but you mean the world to me. I want to take away your pain, but I can't. The people accusing you are nothing, and you are everything. Stand up to them, Dad, and show them you are strong. They will never break you. I don't believe in God because I don't see how he can allow these things to happen to such a good man. But I do believe in hope and faith, and most of all I believe in YOU.

Love, Chloe.

Four days later, the prosecution case collapsed.

Saying the wrong thing

In your own home, your guard may be down. You may be relaxed, even careless – and the most generous, courteous and thoughtful gesture may be ruined by the wrong choice of words.

Take the man whose wife rang a radio programme to complain about the fact that he had been doing some ironing. From what she said, it was clear that until that morning he hadn't picked up an iron for several years.

So what was wrong with that? Many wives would be delighted to have a husband who does the ironing, even if only rarely. But that wasn't the point.

'It's what he said,' she complained. 'He handed me a pile of ironing that he'd finished and said, "There you are, I've ironed all my shirts for you."'

Don't mention it

It's often said that if you step on somebody's toe on the New York subway, the very least you can expect to receive is a torrent of abuse and invective – while if you do the same thing on the London Underground, your victim will probably apologise for carelessly putting his toe under your foot.

But even in England, few people can shrug off an injury with the same aplomb as the young Thomas Macaulay. At just 4 years old, the future Lord Macaulay – politician, poet and historian – was with his parents on a visit to Lady Waldegrave at Strawberry Hill, near Twickenham, when a careless servant spilled hot coffee over his legs. Instead of crying, screaming or running for his mother, the little boy solemnly replied to Lady Waldegrave's anxious inquiries: 'Thank you, madam, the agony is abated.'

And even he could not compete with the hopefully apocryphal story of a gentleman standing in a London bus queue whose eye was put out by a careless lady wielding an umbrella. 'It's quite all right, madam,' he is reported to have said, dabbing gently at the blood coursing down his cheek, 'I have another'.

Fighting back

There's no reason why politeness should make you a pushover. For some of us, the Holy Grail of courtesy is the comment that allows us to respond to someone else's rudeness in such a way that we keep our composure, maintain our standards and still manage to squash them as flat as if we'd savaged them with words.

But very few of us manage to do that with the wit, flair and simplicity of Baron Hans Guido von Bülow, the famous German Romantic conductor and composer. Brilliant musician though he was, von Bülow's friends might have been surprised to see him quoted as an example of courtesy, since he had a reputation for tactlessness and plain speaking. Once he is said to have told a trombonist playing in his orchestra, 'Your tone sounds like gravy running through a sewer' – but on this occasion, he reached the heights of cool.

It was the sort of simple incident that happens to everyone; climbing a narrow staircase, he collided with another man coming down. 'Idiot!' the stranger shouted at him angrily.

Von Bülow, in reply, simply raised his hat, extended his hand, and made a slight bow. 'Von Bülow,' he said.

He is the unchallenged champion of the civil but crushing riposte – but an anonymous Italian gentleman from the era of Mussolini might rival him for simple courage. When violently jostled by a stranger on a crowded Rome railway station, he turned to remonstrate angrily with his assailant – to find himself staring at the stout, sweating and swaggering figure of Hermann Göring, Hitler's *Reichsmarschall*, and one of the most powerful men in Nazi Germany.

As the Italian, unperturbed, demanded an apology, Göring thrust out his chest aggressively. 'I am Hermann Göring,' he thundered, expecting him to crumble like everyone else he came into contact with. But the Italian was equal to the bully. 'As an excuse, that is not sufficient,' he replied calmly. 'But as an explanation, it is more than enough.'

Stand aside

The dilemma of a pacifist who is threatened with violence is even more stark than that of a courteous man who has to respond to rudeness. But the mild response of the famous nineteenth-century American Quaker, Joseph Whittall, when he woke to find a burglar in his house, demonstrates that gentle words can mask a steely determination.

'Friend,' he said equably, 'I wish thee would stand to one side. I am about to shoot where thee is standing.'

Do I have your attention?

We have all met those annoying people at parties who carry on a conversation while keeping one eye looking out over your shoulder to see if there is anyone more interesting or influential in the room. One of the first rules of courtesy might be that there is nothing and nobody more important than the person with whom you are speaking.

As Sir Michael Adeane, later Baron Adeane, could have testified.

For twenty years, he was principal private secretary to the queen at Buckingham Palace, where one day he was observed walking calmly but purposefully towards the front of the building. The writer Basil Boothroyd, who was researching his biography of Prince Philip, caught sight of him and hurried to intercept him with a question about the work he was doing.

Sir Michael listened carefully as Boothroyd explained his problem at some length – but after several minutes, the writer began to pick up the merest hint that there was something else fighting for his attention, and politely asked if he was detaining him.

'No, no,' said Sir Michael. 'It's just that ... Well, I do hope you'll forgive me, but I've just heard that my house is on fire. It wouldn't matter, but since it is part of St James' Palace ...'

Extreme table manners

The controversial Paul Liebrandt, who has spent ten years as one of New York's most original and avant-garde chefs, has perhaps in the past occasionally overstepped the boundaries of good taste. Combinations of eel and chocolate or onions and sorbet were one thing; inviting his guests to lap up foie gras from their soup with their wrists bound was quite another.

Now, established as a serious and highly respected restaurateur, he dismisses such antics as a part of his early search for publicity – but one stunt won't go away. If you read about Liebrandt, you can't miss the story of the guests who were invited to peel jelly from the back of a naked woman, stretched out along the table in a smoke-filled room.

Today, he shrugs it off. 'Half of them didn't even realise it was a real woman until one guy poked her bum,' he told *Esquire* magazine.

And so what does that have to do with a book about manners and courtesy? Just this: in the unlikely event that you are ever invited to eat your dinner off the back of a naked woman, it is considered the mark of a gentleman to be careful with his fork.

And if you are opening a restaurant, you should remember that the craziest publicity stunts will one day come back to haunt you.

∽

A small mistake

There may be some people who are as polite, courteous and charming behind their own front doors as they are in public – but the Scottish judge Lord Braxfield was not one of them. He was evocatively described by his fellow judge, Lord Cockburn, as being 'strong built and dark, with rough eyebrows, powerful eyes, threatening lips, and a low growling voice, he was like a formidable blacksmith', and his manners matched his appearance.

Braxfield, one of the cruellest judges to sit in Scotland in the eighteenth century – a title for which there was considerable competition – was playing a hand of whist one night when he became annoyed by the way his partner was playing.

'What d'ye think ye're doing, ye damned auld bitch!' he growled at her – and then, suddenly collecting his thoughts and squinting across the table, added: 'Your pardon's begged, madam. I took ye for my ain wife.'

It's only fair to the judge to point out that even outside his own family circle, his manners were not particularly gentle. His favourite maxim, uttered whenever prosecutors suggested that there may not be legal grounds for punishing supposed enemies of King George, was 'Let them bring me prisoners, and I'll find 'em law', and he worked long and hard to justify his reputation as the Hanging Judge.

Giving up your seat for a lady

Bringing up children is one of the most challenging of tasks, and teaching them manners may be one of the hardest parts – especially if they sometimes may have reason to doubt your own motives. Take the case of the American writer, poet and humorist Oliver Herford, who was riding on a bus one day with his young nephew.

The bus was crowded, and Herford had the boy on his lap, when an attractive young woman got on. There was no seat for her, so she had to stand. 'Get up, lad, and offer the lady your seat,' Herford urged the boy.

It's not known whether the boy did as he was told – or if he did, what sort of response he received.

A soft answer

Richard Tapper Cadbury, nineteenth-century father of the founder of the famous chocolate manufacturers, was a kindly, gentle and unfailingly courteous man – but instead of aggression, he had a ready wit and a quick tongue.

Walking through Birmingham one day in his homespun Quaker clothes, he came face to face on a narrow pavement with a sumptuously turned out dandy, who looked for a moment with a supercilious smile at the older man's simple dress and humble demeanour. 'I don't step aside for fools,' drawled the dandy.

Cadbury smiled. 'But I do,' he said pointedly – and stepped aside.

A tipping dilemma

Early in the last century, the American writer and academic Rufus Jones was entertaining a rather grand English friend at his home in Haverford, Pennsylvania. Each night, like a true aristocrat, his guest left his shoes outside his bedroom door so that the maid could clean them.

Jones, however, who lived in a simple and unpretentious style, had no servants in his house – and so each night, he quietly took the shoes and polished them himself.

On the morning when he was leaving, his guest put a hand in his pocket. 'Here is a dollar – would you pass it on to the girl who cleans the shoes?' he asked. Jones, unwilling to embarrass his guest, nodded and took the money. 'I'll see that she gets it,' he said.

A sentimental moment

Especially when we are talking to children, courtesy or kindness can sometimes descend almost imperceptibly into sentimentality – which is dangerous, because children can be the most unsentimental of creatures. Take the case of an old friend who had the misfortune to see his 10-year-old daughter injured while she was skiing.

He tried to comfort her as she lay helplessly on the snow, waiting for the paramedics to arrive with the ominously-named 'blood wagon', and then, a little later, followed as they skied down the mountain with her strapped to a stretcher between them. In fact, she had simply twisted her knee – a painful accident, but one that caused no lasting damage – but he didn't know that at the time.

That afternoon, with her leg strapped and bandaged after a lengthy session in the doctor's surgery and with everyone else away on the slopes, they sat and drank large mugs of hot chocolate together in the resort. My friend felt an almost physical pain of his own as he remembered her pale shocked face in the minutes after the collision. 'You know,' he said, 'when I saw you lying in the snow this morning, I would have given anything for it to have been me rather than you that was hurt.'

She looked back at him with big, wide, honest eyes. 'Me too,' she said.

The importance of a smile

Simple, everyday courtesy doesn't have to be complicated – but it's hard to exaggerate how important it can sometimes be. There was a man in his thirties who leapt to his death from San Francisco's Golden Gate Bridge, which enjoys the melancholy accolade of being America's premier location for suicides. Only twenty-eight of the more than 1,300 people who are known to have jumped into the swirling waters of the Pacific nearly 750ft below have survived; remorseless currents carry the bodies of many of the dead out to sea, and they are never found.

This man's body was recovered, however, and the police were able to trace where he had been staying. They went there to see if they could find any information about his background or his identity, and discovered a note he had left behind.

In it, he said that he was going to the bridge to end his life – but that if a single person smiled at him as he was on his way he would turn around and come home. Clearly, nobody did.

A late-night altercation

One of the many stories which the great French playwright Alexandre Dumas, *fils* – son of the famous novelist – most enjoyed hearing told about himself involved his serene handling of a small conjugal difficulty. He had returned unexpectedly from a ball, which he had attended alone, to find his wife, Ida, already in bed. It was winter, and the rest of the house was freezing cold, although there was a roaring fire in her bedroom. So, ignoring Ida's protestations that she wanted to be left alone to sleep, he sat down to read for a little while in front of the fire.

After a few minutes the door to Ida's private bathroom was suddenly flung open with a crash, and Dumas' friend Roger de Beauvoir – a Romantic novelist with a great reputation as a ladies' man – burst into the room, wearing nothing but his shirt. 'This is very embarrassing,' he said, 'but I'm freezing to death in there while you warm yourself by the fire.'

Men had fought duels with less provocation, and Dumas was understandably shocked and furious. There was an angry exchange, at the end of which he began to manhandle the interloper out of his house. When he opened the door to an icy blast of wind, however, and saw the rain pelting down, he paused; de Beauvoir was an old friend, after all, it was a bitter night and in any case, he and his wife were not particularly close. They did, after all, have separate bedrooms. More to the point, perhaps, Dumas had a certain reputation of his own. It could, he reasoned, have been him hiding in the darkness in a strange bathroom.

He shut the door again, and ushered de Beauvoir back into the room. 'We'll discuss this tomorrow,' he said. 'For the time being, you take my chair by the fire, and I'll get into bed.'

But as the fire died down and de Beauvoir huddled closer and closer to the embers, the noise of his chattering teeth and shivering woke Dumas again. 'Oh, come to bed,' he shouted, and de Beauvoir slipped between the sheets on the other side of Ida – and so they stayed, with Dumas' wife either sleeping or pretending to sleep soundly with her husband on one side and her lover on the other.

Dumas was the first to wake, and leaning over his wife, he shook de Beauvoir by the shoulder. 'I've been thinking,' he said. 'Why should old friends break up over a woman, even a wife?'

Perhaps, for modern tastes, this was taking courtesy a little far, and maybe Ida's opinion might have been canvassed. But Dumas certainly had style.

The odd couple

Marriage can be entered into for all sorts of reasons: love, lust, social ambition or simple financial greed. Sometimes, as in the case of Erika Mann and W.H. Auden, it can be a matter of kindness and generosity, mixed with the need to outwit a tyrannical government.

In 1935 the 30-year-old Mann, a popular actress and writer, was threatened with the loss of her German citizenship in retaliation for her role in devising *The Pepper Mill*, a satirical cabaret review which ridiculed the Nazi regime. She was gay, and she appealed to her friend and fellow-homosexual, the novelist Christopher Isherwood, to marry her so that she could obtain an English passport.

Isherwood was unwilling to help, but he described her plight to Auden, who immediately agreed to become her husband. Since he was also homosexual, the marriage between the two partners – who had not even met until a few days before the ceremony – was a complete sham, but it enabled Mann to escape from Nazi Germany and the two became good friends when they were living in New York.

Erika went on to make arrangements for scores of other artists, political dissidents and enemies of the Nazis to escape, and on one occasion approached Auden again. Could he find another homosexual man to help another actress, like herself, who was under threat and needed a foreign passport because of her anti-Nazi activities? Auden found a friend who cheerfully obliged, and another anti-Nazi activist was saved from probable imprisonment and death.

Auden himself affected not to understand why Erika was so grateful. 'After all, what are buggers for?' he asked cheerfully.

Marks of mutual respect

The controversial Tory politician Enoch Powell could be impatient, even irascible, but in his personal relationships, he was punctilious about good manners. In the 1980s, the Irish-born Conservative journalist, writer and political polemicist Patrick Cosgrave (1941–2001) was commissioned to write his official biography, for which Powell granted him access to his files of correspondence. This entailed Cosgrave visiting Powell at his house in London, where a room had been set aside for him to work in. There he found all the paraphernalia a writer might need: desk and chair, paper and writing implements, files of documents he might want to consult, plus he also had access to Powell himself.

Both were courteous men, but Powell passionately disliked smoking, whereas Patrick smoked heavily. On the desk each day, Cosgrave would find a clean ashtray. On the desk each evening, when the writer left, Powell would also find a clean and unused ashtray. Each man, consistently, silently and generously, deferred to the wishes of the other. This is, it's true, only a small story, but it speaks much for their mutual respect.

The kindness of strangers

Dom Joly was the star of the wildly successful *Trigger Happy TV*, a hidden-camera comedy series that ran on British TV for two series in 2000 and 2001. In October 2008, in one of his weekly columns in *The Independent on Sunday*, the British television comedian and journalist Joly told of the kindness of a stranger in Los Angeles as the world's financial crisis continued to deepen.

He was filming a sketch in the middle of the banking district of the city, playing the part of a desperate and bedraggled financial trader. He stood in the street, apparently lost. His business suit was dishevelled, his briefcase was hanging wide open and empty, and there was a panic-stricken look in his eyes. He was clearly a victim of the credit crunch. Nervous bankers crossed the street to avoid him and turned their faces away, as if by speaking to him, touching him or even passing close by him they might somehow be infected by his bad luck. But then, suddenly, one of them broke ranks and came over to him.

'Hey buddy, you OK?' he asked with a look of deep concern. Joly was too embarrassed to admit that he was acting a part; the Good Samaritan had clearly not noticed the film camera with the huge zoom lens on the other side of the street, and Joly was not going to point it out to him.

'I ... lost my job today, they just came and said it was all over ... I've got nothing.'

Joly was throwing his heart and soul into the performance. His new friend smiled softly.

'Don't worry, buddy, the whole country is going through a tough time right now but we'll get through it. We've just got to stand together. I lost my job two years back but I got it together and so will you. What sector are you in, do you want some lunch? Maybe I can help you?'

Joly was staggered – it was an extraordinary gesture of random and completely unexpected generosity. Banking crisis or no banking crisis, Joly concluded, all is definitely not lost in the USA.

4

THE GREAT &
THE GOOD

By and large, diplomats, politicians, government ministers and other pillars of society don't get a very good press. All too often their jobs involve protecting their dignity, and it is easy for them to seem pompous and self-important. But when they are not dealing with great matters of public policy or kept at a distance by officials or press secretaries, they feel ordinary emotions and they speak to ordinary people.

Beneath their crowns, chains of office or diplomatic honours, they have the same faults and virtues as everybody else, and a flash of humour, a moment's generosity or even an ironic raised eyebrow can sometimes reveal a real person who may be much more human than anyone ever guessed.

Throughout history, those who have held high office may often have had an inflated idea of their own importance; they may have seemed stiff and unapproachable, and their motives may sometimes have been questionable. But when their ordinary human kindness does show through, it's hard to doubt the sincerity of courtesy which is extended to those from whom they need neither fear injury nor hope for gain from.

Your obedient enemy

Sometimes, extravagant courtesy can be used to make a point, as in the case of Winston Churchill and his punctilious little note of December 1941 to the Japanese ambassador, declaring war. No doubt it was partly the result of having 'the right way to behave' drummed into him as a child – but the story, told in the Commons, also enabled him to score several very public points for cool and confidence. The note read as follows:

> Sir,
>
> On the evening of December 7th His Majesty's Government in the United Kingdom learned that Japanese forces without previous warning either in the form of a declaration of war or of an ultimatum with a conditional declaration of war had attempted a landing on the coast of Malaya and bombed Singapore and Hong Kong.
>
> In view of these wanton acts of unprovoked aggression committed in flagrant violation of International Law and particularly of Article I of the Third Hague Convention

relative to the opening of hostilities, to which both Japan and the United Kingdom are parties, His Majesty's Ambassador at Tokyo has been instructed to inform the Imperial Japanese Government in the name of His Majesty's Government in the United Kingdom that a state of war exists between our two countries.

I have the honour to be, with high consideration, Sir,

Your obedient servant,

Winston S. Churchill

Churchill was criticised for his extravagantly respectful words. However, he later wrote of it, 'Some people did not like this ceremonial style. But after all, when you have to kill a man, it costs nothing to be polite'.

A most superior person

Occasionally, demonstrations of courtesy are so extreme that the suspicion arises that they may not be entirely sincerely meant. Even the most exalted figures in public life may not be above sarcasm. Take the case of the Earl of Derby and the Honourable George Nathaniel, First Marquess Curzon of Kedleston.

The marquess was every bit as grand as his name suggests. As a young student at Oxford in the 1870s, he was lampooned by his contemporaries in the famous rhyme:

My name is George Nathaniel Curzon,
I am a most superior person.

Perhaps the impression of stiffness and pomposity were partly the result of his having to wear a rigid corset because of a spinal injury – or perhaps he was simply an unmitigated and self-important snob. In any case, his appointment as Viceroy to India at the age of 39, and then as Foreign Secretary, did nothing to make him more humble. He delighted in laying down the law to other mortals on all manner of subjects; 'Gentlemen never wear brown in town' was one of his pronouncements. As was his famous advice to his new wife about making love: 'The lady never moves.'

When he was Foreign Secretary even the Prime Minister, David Lloyd George, and his Cabinet colleagues got the full Curzon treatment. He suffered from phlebitis, and would sit grandly in Cabinet meetings with his leg resting on a green baize footstool. Several times, ministers were kept waiting for him with no message, no apology and no explanation.

Eventually, it was too much for the Earl of Derby, Lloyd George's Secretary for War, who was every bit as self-important as Curzon but with a rather more well-developed sense of humour. When a servant arrived, gravely carrying the famous green footstool, and placed it before the Foreign Secretary's empty chair, the noble earl rose to his feet. Bowing solemnly to the footstool, he declared: 'The Marquess himself has not arrived, but we see premonitory symptoms'.

A matter of honour

In modern politics, no quarter is asked for or given. If a minister's carelessness or indiscretion hands the opposition a stick with which to beat him, he can confidently expect a sound and public thrashing, either in parliament, in the newspapers or on television. It was not always so.

Sir Robert Peel and Benjamin Disraeli, two giants of the Conservative Party in nineteenth-century politics, loathed each other. In Disraeli's case, this dislike went back to a perceived slight when he had written a private letter to Peel in an unsuccessful plea for a place in his government. His wife added her own personal appeal, with the rider, 'Be pleased not to answer this, as I do not wish any human being to know I have written to you this humble petition'.

The letters were indeed unanswered, and Disraeli received no promotion. This rebuff rankled for several years, and he frequently turned his lacerating wit on the Conservative prime minister. Four years later, provoked beyond endurance, Peel snapped back during a House of Commons debate that Disraeli's criticism came ill from a man who had once been 'ready, as I think he was, to unite his fortunes with mine in office'.

Inexplicably, Disraeli replied with a flat lie. 'I can say that I have never asked a favour of the Government ... With respect to my being a solicitor for office, it is entirely unfounded,' he said. He must have known of the existence of the two letters that would prove he was lying; even as he spoke, he must have realised that he was handing Peel a weapon with which the prime minister could destroy him.

And Peel said – nothing. He merely repeated his original comment, without mentioning the existence of the letters. A political victory was one thing, but reading out personal and private correspondence in public would have been dishonourable and beneath him. It was a matter not just of courtesy to an undeserving political opponent, but of personal honour. Only after more than fifty years, when both men were dead, were the letters finally made public.

Popping the question

There are disadvantages to high position. The dignity of one's office may create a distance from other people that may not always be welcome – and if this is true today, it was even more so in Queen Victoria's time. The trick, even for a young and inexperienced woman and even for a monarch as concerned with propriety as Victoria, was to sweep away the conventions when they threatened to get in the way.

In December 1830, the 21-year-old queen was about to inform the Privy Council of her decision to marry Prince Albert of Saxe-Coburg and Gotha. One of the ladies of her court, the Duchess of Gloucester, asked her whether such a solemn announcement did not make her feel nervous.

'Not at all,' the queen replied. 'But it was a nervous thing to propose to Prince Albert.'

'What! Did *you* propose to *him*?' asked the duchess, as shocked as it is permissible to be with one's sovereign.

'To be sure I did,' said the queen. 'He would never have taken such a liberty as to propose to the Queen of England.'

This momentous act of courtesy by the young queen to her future husband – who was himself only 20 years old at the time – led to a marriage that produced nine children, and which remained close and passionate until his death at the early age of 42.

Things were done much better

Queen Alexandra, the consort of King Edward VII, behaved with impeccable dignity throughout her married life, as scandal after scandal about her husband's affairs with actresses, singers, court ladies and members of London's demi-monde were whispered about and hushed up.

As the king lay dying, she welcomed his last mistress, Alice Keppel, to the little group at his death bed. Great-great-grandmother of the present Duchess of Cornwall, Keppel was a well-known courtesan with a list of past lovers that looked like a page from Debrett's. The king was the latest of a long line of aristocratic lovers to share her favours.

But Queen Alexandra, who was well aware of her liaison with Edward, shook her by the hand. 'I am sure you always had a good influence on him,' she said gently.

Alice Keppel, incidentally, was clearly appreciative of Alexandra's forbearance and courtesy. Nearly three decades later, whilst dining at the Ritz, the 70-year-old *grande horizontale* was told that her lover's grandson, King Edward VIII, was abdicating the throne to marry his lover, Wallis Simpson. 'Things were done much better in my day,' she observed.

Being nice to Hitler

In today's era of cocksure television presenters, it may be hard to think of the BBC as the sober-sided mouthpiece of the nation, desperate to avoid causing offence. Back in the thirties, though, these things mattered – sometimes, perhaps, a little too much.

The comedian Ronald Frankau, descended from a German Jewish family, submitted a song which he planned to sing in a BBC broadcast, containing the words 'Let's find Hitler and kick him in the pants'. BBC executives decided, after consulting the Foreign Office, that it might be found offensive by the German Chancellor.

Might it be possible to drop Hitler's name, and substitute 'Carnera' – the name of an Italian heavyweight boxer – they suggested, apparently not noticing that the new line would not scan, would not be funny and would not make sense. Men who sit in offices seldom have a sense of humour.

Frankau certainly did not find their suggestion funny, and the song was never performed – but the BBC retained its reputation for politeness and courtesy, and no offence was caused to Adolf Hitler or the Nazis.

Bearing a grudge

In their official capacity, members of the Royal Family always try to avoid disputes. It would be discourteous in the extreme, for instance, to tell a guest at a royal function that he is talking rubbish – far better to say something bland and avoid controversy.

However, they don't need actually to agree. So maybe the late Queen Mother went a little far when she was introduced to a leathery-skinned old Boer farmer from South Africa at a garden party.

'I can never forgive the English for the way they raped and occupied my country,' he said – still unsmiling, some eighty years after the end of the Boer War.

The Queen Mother smiled indulgently. 'I quite understand,' she replied conspiratorially. 'We feel much the same in Scotland.'

Lost in translation

Occasionally, just occasionally, it may be necessary to sacrifice truth in order to preserve courtesy. Her Highness Princess Charlotte Sophia of Mecklenburg-Strelitz, who travelled to London in 1761 to marry the young King George III, was not, to put it kindly, conventionally pretty. She had a wide, flat face, big ears, a large mouth and a snub pug nose – in fact, although King George's courtiers would have been much too polite to suggest it, it was generally agreed that she looked like a dog.

The crowds who thronged the streets to see her coach pass by, however, did not share the reticence of the court. 'Pug!' they shouted. 'Pug!'

The princess, whose grasp of English was as limited as her beauty, turned to her lady-in-waiting, the Duchess of Ancaster. 'Vat is this vord they are saying? Vat means *poog*?'

Without a pause, the duchess replied, tactfully but maybe not entirely convincingly: 'It means "God bless Your Royal Highness."'

The story, like the London crowd, is less than fair to the princess, who was not only a keen and dedicated amateur botanist, but also a noted patron of the arts. She was also a loyal consort to King George and bore him fifteen children, remaining at his side throughout the illness which left him, in the poet Shelley's cruel words, 'an old, mad, blind, despised and dying king'.

A gentle reminder

A young European diplomat was invited to dinner with Grover Cleveland, twenty-second and twenty-fourth President of the United States, and his wife Frances Folsom Cleveland during Cleveland's second term of office in the 1890s. Cleveland was the only president ever to be voted out of office and then return to the White House for a second term – and also the only president to be married while in office. His wife, who was renowned for her beauty and good humour, and who became one of the most popular first ladies ever to live in the White House, was only 21 when they married in 1886 during his first term, but she developed a clear eye for social etiquette.

Their young dinner guest was about to tuck into the salad with which he had been served when he noticed a large and particularly unpleasant-looking worm lurking under a leaf. He was about to call one of the staff to point this out when he caught Mrs Cleveland's eye, observing him narrowly. Nothing was said, not even an eyebrow was raised, but her meaning was clear; any complaint would not go down well with the president.

The diplomat meekly ate his salad, worm and all. The First Lady nodded and smiled. 'Young man, you will go a long way,' she said. Fifteen years later he returned to Washington, not as a junior diplomat, but as his country's ambassador.

Punctuality & the politeness of kings

King George V always insisted on strict punctuality, particularly at mealtimes – the royal family were expected to sit down together each evening for a formal dinner. Nothing annoyed the king more than lateness at the table.

At the same time, however, King George was very fond of his new daughter-in-law, the former Elizabeth Bowes-Lyon. She was later to be King George VI's Queen Elizabeth, and subsequently the universally respected Queen Mother – but on this occasion, only in her twenties and the new wife of the king's second son, she committed the cardinal sin of arriving late in the royal dining room.

She apologised profusely and waited nervously as everyone anticipated an explosion of wrath from the notoriously short-tempered king. Instead he smiled indulgently, ostentatiously consulted his pocket watch, and said: 'You are not late, my dear. I think we must have sat down two minutes early.'

Don't stand on ceremony

The mark of a true gentleman is that he inspires respect without ever seeming to try to do so. Henry Kissinger,

American Secretary of State under President Richard Nixon, however, could be a stickler for etiquette. At an official reception, impatient with the nervous dithering of a young guest, he growled, 'I never stand on protocol. Just call me Your Excellency.'

Much the same thing happened to the future Poet Laureate, John Betjeman, as a young man when he became engaged to his future wife Penelope Chetwode. Her parents did not approve of the match, but her father, Field Marshall Lord Chetwode of the Indian army, made what he clearly thought was a generous conciliatory gesture. 'Well Betjeman,' he barked to the nervous suitor, 'if you're going to be my son-in-law, you needn't go on calling me "Sir". Just call me "Field Marshal".'

❧

Follow that car

The American politician and diplomat Averell Harriman held high office under several American presidents, and was ambassador to the Soviet Union in the final years of the Second World War, before coming to London as ambassador in 1946. Although the Americans and the Russians were allies in the fight against Hitler, the KGB had orders from Stalin that Harriman was to be kept under close surveillance.

No one bothered to try to hide the fact that he was followed everywhere he went by the secret police. One winter weekend, he set off to visit a British diplomat at his country home outside Moscow, considerately warning the two agents shadowing him that they would need a four-wheel-drive vehicle to negotiate the rough country roads.

The Russians, presumably thinking that they needed no advice from a foreigner about how to cope with the winter weather, ignored his advice and set off after him in their heated but quite unsuitable saloon car. Before long it got bogged down in the mud and snow, as Harriman had warned, so he ordered his driver to slow down so that one of the secret policemen, following on foot, could keep up.

Slowly the official car made its way up the road until Harriman, worried that the Russian might freeze to death and presumably wanting to speed up his own journey, stopped and offered him a ride, promising not to tell anyone about it. The KGB was not known for its sense of humour, and the agent might have faced savage punishment, but the man accepted, and the ambassador and his secret police 'tail' finished the journey sitting side by side in the American Embassy's car. Harriman kept his promise until his memoirs were published some thirty years later.

In fact, the KGB may well have learned about it some time earlier through their own nefarious channels. In 1945 Harriman was presented with a wooden carving of the Great Seal of the United States, which was duly given pride of place in Spaso House – then, as now, the official Moscow residence of the American ambassador. Seven years later, it was found to have been bugged so that the Soviet secret service could eavesdrop on the ambassador's private conversations.

An ambiguous gesture

Thomas Jefferson, the third President of the United States, was a convinced and dedicated abolitionist – but also a lifelong slave-owner. It was a contradiction that he struggled with all his life, and one that biographers still argue about. It is accepted that by the standards of his time, he treated his slaves well, having many of them educated and others trained in practical skills. But he still believed that blacks were by nature inferior to their white masters.

One frequently repeated story describes how he was out in a carriage one day with his grandson near his mountain-top estate of Monticello in Virginia. A slave who was walking in the road, and whom neither Jefferson nor his grandson knew, politely doffed his hat to them. Jefferson, as he always did, took off his own hat and acknowledged the gesture, but his grandson simply kept talking, ignoring the man.

Jefferson turned to him, frowning. 'Do you permit a slave to be more of a gentleman than you are?' he asked severely.

It's possible, reflecting Jefferson's own ambiguity, to see that exchange either as the behaviour of a racist who assumed that his own white family should be superior in every way to the black slaves that they owned, or as that of a man of impeccable courtesy insisting that everyone should be treated with respect. Either way, it was another thirty-five years before the end of America's bloody Civil War settled the question of slavery forever.

The assassin who couldn't shoot

Frenchmen, as everybody knows, are passionate and excitable – or at least that is the stereotype. There is, people occasionally joke, no word in French for sangfroid. But Georges Clemenceau, Prime Minister of France at the end of the First World War, believed that calm composure was first cousin to courtesy.

As preparations were being made for the Treaty of Versailles, which would formally end the war, Clemenceau was fired on in an assassination attempt by a young anarchist, Emile Cottin. Cottin loosed off seven shots from a revolver, grazing the elderly statesman's head with one bullet.

The crowd nearly lynched Cottin, but Clemenceau remarked calmly:

> We have just won the most terrible war in history, yet here is a Frenchman who misses his target six times out of seven. Of course the fellow must be punished for the careless use of a dangerous weapon. Eight years in prison with intensive training in a shooting gallery.

In fact, Cottin was sentenced to death, but later had his sentence commuted to ten years in prison. It is not known whether he managed to improve his shooting. He later died while fighting in the Spanish Civil War.

Free & easy

Whatever else diplomats manage when abroad in a foreign country, they can usually be relied on to get the protocol right – and when they try to bend the rules a little, they can come sadly unstuck.

The journalist Frank Giles, one-time editor of *The Sunday Times*, was travelling abroad with his wife when they were invited to a formal Embassy dinner – some versions of this story say it was the American Embassy, others, the British. The invitation was addressed to Mr and Mrs Frank Giles – which, as Giles' wife Katherine was the daughter of an earl and retained her title, was something of a breach of protocol. She should have been addressed as Lady Katherine Giles.

So Giles rang the Embassy to point out the error. He wasn't complaining, he started gently, but the lady accompanying him wasn't exactly *Mrs* Giles. The member of the Embassy staff at the other end of the phone cut him off in mid-sentence.

'That's OK, don't worry about it,' he said encouragingly. 'Bring her along anyway. We're not a bit stuffy here.'

A gentleman?

John Dalrymple, second Earl of Stair and King George I's ambassador to Paris, was a man with a reputation. He was, the elderly Earl of Chesterfield declared approvingly, the most 'finished' gentleman he ever knew.

This 'finish' – breeding or good taste, in modern terms – held him in good stead. He was a favourite of King Louis XIV, who decided to put his reputedly exquisite manners to an idiosyncratic test. As they got into a carriage together, the king stood aside to allow him to mount the steps first. Without a pause, the earl climbed into the carriage before him. On the face of it, a shocking breach of etiquette, but one that seemed to please the king.

'It is true what I have heard, for this man did not trouble me with ceremony, whereas one less polite, would have stood bowing, and making a thousand excuses and apologies for refusing what I desired,' he said.

On another occasion, the earl was at a dinner where his fellow diplomats were vying with each other in extravagant praise of their monarchs. The French ambassador, the Abbé de Ville, proposed a toast to 'the Rising Sun', by which he meant King Louis. The Austrian ambassador, the Baron de Reisbach, replied with a toast to 'the Moon', referring to the empress. Then it was the Earl of Stair's turn and he, referring to a Biblical verse, proposed a toast to the King of England as 'Joshua, who made the sun and moon stand still'. It was a quip that can have done him no harm at all when repeated back at court in London.

So the earl had the invaluable gifts for a diplomat of wit and charm. But there was, too, a side to his character that may have been less savoury.

He had an enviable reputation for pleasing the ladies of King Louis' court, and playing cards one night, he lent a thousand *louis d'or* to the Duchess of Maine, a relative of the French king and a woman of immense influence who had suffered a run of bad luck. Summoned to see her next day, he brushed aside her pleas that he should say nothing about the loan, which would have been extremely embarrassing to her.

'I had already forgotten it myself, and should never have recollected it again had not Your Highness put my memory to the rack by refreshing it,' he smiled. A characteristically generous and chivalrous gesture, on the face of it – except that soon afterwards, the duchess began passing him important and confidential information. Was it a coincidence, or had she been blackmailed? Or bribed? Either way, it's not an incident that reflects particularly well on the exquisite Earl of Stair.

An aristocrat, perhaps, but not entirely a gentleman.

Grace under pressure

History has not been kind to Marie Antoinette, the queen of Louis XVI of France, who died on the guillotine in the French Revolution. Everybody recalls how when told that the people of Paris were starving and could get no bread, she said '*Qu'ils mangent de la brioche!*' ('Let them eat cake!') – which may or may not be true.

No one has said where or when she made the remark, which sounds like a piece of post-Revolutionary propaganda. It certainly wasn't an original comment –

indeed it was quoted as a current saying at least fifty years before her time.

But in any case, there are other, more believable, stories that show the young French queen in a much more sensitive and courteous light. Probably the most poignant describes her on the scaffold, about to be executed in front of the baying mob.

Stepping towards the guillotine, she accidentally trod on the executioner's foot. Pale and trembling, she turned and bowed slightly towards the man who was about to cut off her head. 'I ask your pardon, Monsieur,' she said. 'I did not do it on purpose.'

The 'Merry Monarch' & the queen who was not amused

William Penn, the founder of the American state of Pennsylvania, was a Quaker and believed passionately in the equality of all men before God – a belief that was commonly put into practice among his fellow Quakers by a refusal to remove their hats when introduced to people.

This minor social embarrassment could have been a serious breach of etiquette when he found himself in the presence of King Charles II – but luckily, the king had a sense of humour. It was not for nothing that he was known as the 'Merry Monarch'. With a flourish and a bow he removed his own hat.

'Friend Charles,' said Penn – the unusual form of address another mark of his Quaker beliefs – 'Why dost thou take off thy hat?'

'Friend Penn,' the king replied, with a smile. 'Dost thou not know that in this place it is the custom that only one man at a time should keep his hat on?'

Queen Victoria, however, was famous for being less easily amused, as the Irish peer Michael William de Courcy, 32nd Baron Kingsale – and thus heir to one of the oldest titles in Britain or Ireland – discovered. He appeared at court and attempted to take advantage of a privilege that had allegedly been granted to his forebears by King John some 600 years earlier: allowing them to appear before the monarch without removing their hats. (Some authorities suggest that if this privilege was ever granted at all, it may well have been because the noble lord's hair was infested with lice.)

The queen looked at him for a moment, nonplussed. Then, when the baron explained the ancient legend, she scoffed. 'Don't be so silly,' she said briskly. 'You may have the right to keep your hat on before your monarch, but I happen to be a lady as well. Take it off at once!'

Confrontation with the emperor

There is no shortage of anecdotes about the great and powerful behaving well. Those, after all, are the one they would like to see repeated. For sheer vulgarity, met with aristocratic good breeding, it is hard to beat the story of Napoleon's confrontation with his Grand Chamberlain, Charles-Maurice de Talleyrand-Périgord.

Talleyrand was a subtle, scheming and serpentine French diplomat and statesman, who had already served under Louis XVI through the French Revolution, and would go on to hold office under Louis XVIII, Charles X and Louis Philippe as well.

There is confusion over what sparked Napoleon's wrath; some accounts say that it was Talleyrand's opposition to his invasion of Spain and Portugal, others that the emperor suspected him of plotting his assassination. What is known, however, is that Napoleon summoned a meeting of his council on 28 January 1809, at which he turned on Talleyrand in the most abusive way.

In front of all the other ministers, he raged and swore at him, finally screaming in his face: '*Tenez, vous êtes de la merde dans un bas do soie!*' ('You're a piece of shit in a silk stocking!') – a forceful but unconventional description. There was a moment's silence as the aristocratic and refined Talleyrand stared at the emperor. Then, as Napoleon stormed out of the room, he murmured disdainfully, 'What a pity that such a great man should be so ill bred!'

That barely disguised contempt, however, did not prevent Talleyrand from continuing to serve Napoleon assiduously – at least until it became clear that the French monarchy was likely to return, at which point he reconciled himself with the surviving exiled members of the Bourbon dynasty. After all, another of his famous sayings was 'Regimes may fall and fail, but I do not'.

An expression of trust

Throughout history, and often with good cause, kings, generals and great leaders have lived their lives in a fog of suspicion, unable to trust even their closest servants. They have been surrounded by guards, with food tasters constantly on call to protect them against the risk of poison. The courts of the mighty were seldom a healthy place to live.

The Greek chronicler Plutarch tells a story about Alexander the Great that demonstrates the atmosphere of fear and distrust that encompassed his followers – and the nobility with which he responded to it.

Marching through Asia Minor on the way to his great victories over the Persians, the emperor fell dangerously ill, possibly as a result of swimming in the icy waters of the River Cydnus. His most respected physicians did not dare to treat him, since they realised that if they failed and Alexander died, they would be accused of having killed him. Only one doctor, Philip the Arcanian, had both the confidence and the courage to attend the ailing emperor. It would be, Philip thought, the highest ingratitude not to try to save his life through fear for his own, and so he brought his drugs and medicines into Alexander's tent.

However, Alexander had received a letter warning him to beware of Philip who, the letter-writer said, had been bribed by the Persian King Darius to poison him. He read it and hid it under his pillow without telling anyone, before summoning Philip to bring his medicine. Alexander took the cup, and as he drank it, he handed Philip the letter.

Philip was both outraged and terrified by the accusation, and threw himself on the ground by Alexander's bed, begging the emperor to trust him – and the response from the sick leader was that he had complete faith in Philip's honour and in his medical skill. The medicine was so powerful that it left Alexander in a coma for a while – which must have been a tense time for Philip – but after three days he was well enough to lead his army again.

A poor harvest

The summer of 1783 in France was cold and wet, and the harvest was correspondingly poor, but because the estates of the wealthy Marquis de Lafayette were so extensive, his barns were still well-filled with wheat. The head bailiff pointed out that with prices at record levels because of the shortages, it would be a good time to sell.

But Lafayette – later to play an important role in the American Revolution and become the firm friend of George Washington – had seen the hungry families in the villages of the Auvergne. 'No, this is a good time to give,' he said.

5

A WORLD ELSEWHERE

The English may sometimes like to pretend that good manners were their gift to the world, but other peoples and other cultures have a very different view. Certainly George Bernard Shaw – an Irishman who enjoyed teasing the English – thought that English courtesy left a lot to be desired.

'We don't bother much about dress and manners in England, because, as a rule, we don't dress well and we've no manners,' says a character in one of his plays.

In fact, the famous British self-confidence and insouciance may come across as something quite different to people in other countries. The contrast between the Americans and the British when travelling abroad, according to one assessment, is that Americans behave as if they own the country, while the British behave as if they don't care who owns the country.

The truth is that every culture has its own idea of the proper way to behave. Sometimes, offence may be taken where none was intended. A businessman whose manner would seem laudably brisk and efficient in London or New York would simply seem brash and vulgar in the Arab world; eating with your fingers at a state banquet in Buckingham Palace would cause outrage, but in Beijing, no one would raise an eyebrow. Diplomatic parties in Thailand sometimes resemble slow waltzes around the room, as western guests stand up close to their Thai hosts to speak to them, leading the Thais to back away gently to preserve their personal space.

These, though, are the details of behaviour. Courtesy – putting oneself imaginatively in someone else's place, behaving with consideration, showing hospitality – is valued everywhere.

A generous man

Wilfred Thesiger, the great Arabian traveller of the twentieth century, was not sentimental about the Arabs. In *Arabian Sands*, his classic account of the crossing of the Empty Quarter, he describes with horror the murder of a young child in a tribal blood feud, and hears an account of a gruesome public execution in Riyadh.

But he had no doubt about the generosity, hospitality and courtesy of the bedu tribesmen with whom he travelled. 'The only society in which I have found nobility is that of the bedu,' he said in an interview, years after his wanderings were over.

Again and again, he describes his generous welcome at the hands of strangers – shopkeepers who greet him, sit with him, send for tea and forget to try to sell him anything; or complete strangers who invite him to lunch or dinner. 'I have wondered sadly what Arabs brought up in this tradition have thought when they visited England; and I have hoped that they realised that we are as unfriendly to each other as we must appear to be to them,' he says.

On one occasion an old man in a torn and scruffy loincloth, clearly a beggar, joined Thesiger and his companions at their camp in the desert. Thesiger – a generous enough man by his own rights – gave him a few coins, but was astonished by the warmth of the welcome offered to the old man by the bedu tribesmen.

They explained quietly to him that the guest was not just a poverty-stricken old man, but a famous member of the Bait Imani tribe, widely respected for his generosity. But how could such a man be so generous, Thesiger wondered, looking at the threadbare clothes, the broken sheath of his old dagger and the sagging skin on the starving body. 'I should not have thought he owned anything to be generous with.'

That's true, the Arab explained: once, their guest had been one of the richest men in the tribe, but now all he owned was a few scrawny goats – not a camel, not a wife, not even a son, since his child had been killed a couple of years before by raiders. 'What happened to his camels?' Thesiger asked, still not understanding. 'Did raiders taken them, or did they die of disease?'

No, nothing like that, came the patient reply. He had given everything away, killing his camels to feed strangers who came to his tent; he was ruined by his own generosity. 'By God, he is generous!' the bedu tribesman said, and Thesiger, understanding at last, could hear the envy in his voice.

❧

The blind eye of a gentleman

The Arabs still value the idea of generosity. A western girl, some years ago, was hurrying to her job as a newsreader at Qatar Television, in the Gulf, when she had to stop for petrol. After paying for her fuel, she reversed her heavy four-wheel-drive so that she could leave the petrol station in such haste that she failed to notice the large and shiny Mercedes that had pulled in behind her.

Crash! Her car, with its big no-nonsense bumpers, was unmarked, but the front of the Mercedes was a mangled mess of bent chrome and dented paintwork.

Flustered and embarrassed, she got out to apologise to the driver, an elderly white-robed Arab. 'I'm terribly sorry, the accident was entirely my fault,' she said – slightly unnecessarily, since his car had been stationary when she had hit it. 'I'm afraid I can't stop because I'm late for work, but these are my details.'

Ignoring her proffered card, he looked at the mangled remains of the front of his car. 'Accident?' he said. 'What accident? You should get on your way into work.'

All right, she was young and pretty, and he was clearly rich enough to be able to afford gestures like that. But it was still an act of kindness and courtesy that she remembered for a very long time.

❦

Homeward bound

Thomas Nuttall was a pioneering botanist and zoologist who left his native England early in the nineteenth century to study the flora and fauna of the remote areas of northwest America. His reputation as a scientist was exemplary – he brought back many specimens that were previously unknown to science, and wrote several classic studies of his discoveries – but his standing as an explorer is less sure.

Nuttall suffered from the considerable disadvantage of being unable to find his way. On one plant-hunting expedition he found himself hopelessly lost, and then, terrified by the stories he had heard of savage tribes living in the area, he ran away from the search party which had been sent to find him. He evaded them for three days, until – quite by chance – he stumbled back into camp, with his would-be rescuers hard on his heels.

His fears of attack by the Native Americans were probably justified – the tribes were extremely hostile to incursions into their area. However, when he lost his way in the forest again, he owed his life to the tribesman who found him.

The Native American hunter stumbled upon Nuttall when he had already been lost for hours, and was exhausted and almost unconscious. The great explorer looked so helpless that, rather than scalping the white man and stealing his equipment, he carried him 3 miles to the river, placed him gently in a canoe, and – no doubt wondering how a man who got lost so easily had found his way this far – paddled him back to rejoin the other members of the scientific expedition at their camp.

Unfortunately, the name of this selfless and compassionate rescuer is not recorded. It would be nice to think that, if he ever needed help from the explorers who were trekking through his country, he might have had similar treatment.

The warmest of welcomes

Courtesy and hospitality towards strangers in different times and different places may take forms that would seem bizarre to a twenty-first-century European – but there is no reason to suppose that they were not genuinely meant, and very little doubt that they were extremely well received. Take the story of the Tibetans, told by Marco Polo some 700 years ago.

Tibetan men, he says, prefer to marry women of wide and varied sexual experience – and so when foreigners pass through their country, mothers from miles around hurry to their camp, bringing with them their young and nubile daughters. In a ceremony which sounds rather like some fantasy dreamed up by the editor of a top-shelf lads' magazine, the travellers simply choose the ones they find most attractive, and send the others home disappointed.

The girls then stay with them for as long as they remain in camp; the only rule is that they cannot be taken away. After the travellers have 'worked their will', as Marco Polo delicately puts it, they move on, each one leaving his chosen *inamorata* to return to her village with some small token or trinket to hang around her neck.

To have any chance of catching a suitable husband, the young girls have to build up a collection of twenty or more of these tokens – this gets more and more like the lads' magazine – so there is considerable competition among the girls to gain a place in camp. The girls – at least as far as Marco Polo can see – are happy; the Tibetan men are presumably well pleased with what their future wives have learned. And as for the travellers – well, says Marco Polo, slightly unnecessarily, 'Obviously the country is a fine one to visit for a lad from sixteen to twenty-four.'

Clash of cultures

The one-time Soviet leader Nikita Khrushchev was fond of reminding foreign dignitaries of the many and various cultures that existed under the Soviet umbrella – and particularly of the Cossack tradition of hospitality in the Caucasus. A guest in your home, sharing your bread and salt, should be treated with the greatest hospitality, even if he is your bitter enemy, he used to say. 'But once he steps outside your door, then you can slit his throat.'

Many of the Cossacks had, of course, opposed the Communist revolution from the beginning; many had fought alongside the Nazis against Soviet troops in the Second World War. So maybe Khrushchev was biased against them. In any case, it hardly lay in his mouth to offer lectures on civility – he was known for his rough temper and furious rages.

During debates at the United Nations General Assembly in 1960, when the atmosphere was tense after the shooting down of an American U2 spy plane over Russia, he repeatedly interrupted proceedings by thumping on the desk with his fist and shouting angrily at the speakers.

When a delegate from the Philippines accused the Soviets of imperialism in Eastern Europe, Khrushchev famously took off his shoe and hammered it repeatedly on the desk, almost drowning out the delegate's speech. In response, Britain's urbane and aristocratic Prime Minister Harold Macmillan reportedly murmured: 'Might we have a translation of that?'

A broad hint

Winston Churchill often used his wit and charm to get his way – but even he could not win every time. As the Second

World War neared its end, he was in Yalta with Joseph Stalin and Franklin D. Roosevelt. The purpose of the conference was, of course, to draw up an agreed map of the post-war world – but as the three leaders wrestled with these matters of international diplomacy, Churchill had set his heart upon a personal gift.

The British delegation was housed in the magnificent Alubka Palace, which looks out over the Black Sea, and Churchill had several times stood and admired a great marble statue of a lion in the grounds. It lay as if half-asleep, its head resting on its front paws, and it is not too much to suppose that the British Prime Minister had enough vanity to see something of himself in the magnificent creature.

In a suitably roundabout way, during a pause in the negotiations, Churchill raised the possibility of the statue being offered as a gift. Commenting on the fine craftsmanship and the noble bearing of the lion, he paused for a moment. He understood, he said, that there was a Russian tradition of offering the finest things in the country to show the sincerity of the welcome that was extended to an honoured guest.

But Stalin was too quick for him. 'Indeed,' he said. 'And the finest thing that we have in Russia is socialism.'

The lion stayed in Yalta.

A gift to an unknown beggar

Mohandas Karamchand Gandhi, the renowned Indian independence leader, was universally revered among hundreds of millions of Hindus as Mahatma Gandhi, or 'Great Soul' – and he retained an openhearted kindliness that transcended courtesy.

The story is still told in India of the day that he was being helped on to a train, clad only in his homespun *dhoti* and simple sandals. As the train moved off, one of his sandals slipped off his foot and on to the track below. Without pausing, Gandhi bent down, took the sandal off his other foot, and tossed it out of the train as well. His companions couldn't understand why he should have done such a thing, until he explained.

'Now, the poor man who finds the sandal I have lost will find another one as well, so he will have a pair to wear,' he said.

A regal gesture

As Ibn Saud, the first King of Saudi Arabia, became an old man, age and the wealth of his country's newly discovered oil wells meant that he travelled only in cars rather than by horse or camel – but he was delighted when, on a visit to the hot springs of the oasis town of Hofuf, a local dignitary offered him the gift of a handsome grey stallion.

Like his people, he valued the Arab tradition of generosity, but he also knew that it was important for him to repay the compliment. He summoned his vizier, and called for the massive leather-bound ledger in which were recorded details of the gifts he intended to bestow upon his subjects.

In it, he inscribed the name of the man who had given him the horse, and alongside wrote the sum of 300 riyals which, being considerably more than the horse was worth, would be a fitting way to mark his gratitude and demonstrate his own largesse in return. But unfortunately, as he wrote the nib of his pen caught slightly on the paper, sending a shower of tiny ink blots over the page. The Arabic symbol for a zero is a dot rather than a 0, and the accident had turned the king's 300 riyals into 300,000.

The vizier, commendably careful for his master's wealth, pointed out the error. The king studied the page carefully. 'I see that I have written 300,000 riyals, and that is what you must pay,' he said. 'It is the writing of my hand. Let no man say that the hand of Ibn Saud is more generous than his heart.'

❧

The way of the world

One good friend, on holiday in Syria, was struck by the general friendliness and courtesy of the people. In Damascus, people would spot him in the street as a European, and smile broadly and say, 'Welcome to Syria'. Children would wave excitedly, and old men would look up from their hubble-bubble pipes with a smile.

No doubt they wanted to practise their English; after all, there are not many tourists in Syria – but the good humour and the welcome were clearly genuine.

Sometimes, however, courtesy may not be all it seems. On the same trip, my friend took a taxi with his wife, who worked for the BBC, and they were impressed again by the outspoken friendliness of the driver. What did they think of his country, he asked them, in perfect English. What were they going to see? And then suddenly, as they started to tell him about their experiences, he broke out in a passionate tirade against the government.

Ministers were corrupt, he said – 'Look, here is the special shop where only they can buy goods' – and the poor were cheated at every turn. The police were brutal and they took bribes – all charges which my friend and his wife were well aware had also been made by various international organisations. Then the taxi-driver stopped the car, and there were tears in his eyes.

'My heart is bursting,' he said. 'It is so good to be able to speak openly. My son' – and here he pulled a photograph of a little boy from his pocket – 'I hope my son will grow up in a better country than this.' He wouldn't take a fare, he said, because he had been so happy to be able to talk about his feelings, and it was only with difficulty that my friend persuaded him to take a 'present' for his son, which was about the cost of the journey plus a fair-sized tip.

It was a truly moving encounter for them, and they told the Syrian friend with whom they were staying all about it that night.

'Hmm,' she said. 'It's nice that he should be so interested in you. But you say you told him that you work for the BBC? Funny that a taxi driver should speak such perfect English. Most of them are informers for the secret police.'

So had my friend and his wife been speaking to a free-thinking parent who loved his son and yearned for freedom, or a cold, calculating and cynical secret police informer wanting to know what a couple of journalists were doing in Syria? He has never known.

6

THE SOCIAL WHIRL

Noblesse oblige is an interesting and unusual phrase; a reminder that social standing carries obligations as well as entitlements. If your rank gets you to the front of the queue, it implies you ought to be prepared to do something to earn the privilege.

It goes even further than the old line that all our mothers taught us about treating others in the way that we would expect to be treated: *noblesse oblige* means that we set our own high standards, and however other people may treat us, we will treat them with courtesy and consideration.

It's not always a popular idea; there are plenty of tales of pompous, self-important aristocrats whose only concern is that they should be shown the deference to which they think they should be entitled. At every level of society, we've all met the bores, bullies and buffoons who believe that the party is being held just so that they can show off and monopolise the floor.

But there are others stories of subtlety, kindness and good humour that deserve not to be forgotten. Here are a few of them – together with one or two to remind us of the prickly way in which people may sometimes fall short of the highest standards.

Confrontation on board *Britannia*

Maybe the best way to work out how one should treat one's guests is to imagine how the queen would handle any difficult situation. Royalists and republicans alike seem to agree that she never puts a foot wrong.

On one occasion, she was entertaining President Reagan and his wife at dinner as guests of honour on the royal yacht *Britannia*. In a startling break with royal protocol, she announced that she herself would serve the coffee, and dismissed the stewards. Most people served personally with their coffee by the queen would accept whatever was offered – but the president waved her away. 'No thanks. Do you have a decaff?' he asked airily.

The steward was recalled, and the president's order for decaffeinated coffee was sent off to the kitchens. But President Reagan hadn't finished. He reached out a hand and affectionately patted the queen on her bottom. 'Thanks for taking care of that,' he said.

The queen is a stickler for correct behaviour, and nobody, but nobody, touches her, ever. Aghast, the other guests waited for her response to this piece of trans-Atlantic *lèse-majesté*. Icy, angry or contemptuous, it was hard to imagine how an embarrassing incident could be avoided.

'That's perfectly all right, Mr President,' she smiled. And everyone breathed a sigh of relief.

Taking tea with the queen

Even at Buckingham Place, everything does not always go according to plan. When the queen entertained the victorious England World Cup rugby team for high tea – not being a drink that many of the players were particularly familiar with – the team's hooker Mark Regan was approached by a palace servant wearing scarlet livery with gold frogging on his coat and a tray in his hands.

'Earl Grey, sir?' he said.

Regan, taken slightly by surprise but determined to do the right thing, bowed slightly. 'Mark Regan, your lordship,' he replied smartly.

That, at least, is what Simon Shaw, another member of the team, says. And since he is 6ft 9in tall and weighs over 19 stone, few people argue with him.

Bomb? What bomb?

Sometimes courtesy may be about nothing more or less than refusing to be diverted from the matter in hand. If people have gathered for a particular purpose, it would be unpardonable rudeness to allow oneself to be distracted.

At the height of the Blitz, the Duke of Devonshire was presiding over a committee meeting at the exclusive Pratt's Club in London, which had been called to discuss the election of new members.

Halfway through the proceedings, there was a massive explosion nearby, bringing down the ceiling in a shower of plaster and extinguishing all the lights. After a few minutes, fresh lights were brought and the duke, slightly dishevelled and dusty, blinked around the committee table.

'I can't remember – did we elect the feller or not?' he inquired.

The perfect host

The statesman, financier and imperialist Cecil Rhodes is a controversial figure; remembered by some as a bully and a racist in Africa, and by others as the philanthropic founder of the Rhodes scholarships that have brought thousands of scholars from all over the world to Oxford University. One story frequently told about him, however, suggests that he was a man who knew how to be a host.

He had invited friends to dinner at his mansion in Kimberley, and they were all gathered in dinner jackets waiting for their host to appear. There was a nervous knock at the door and the last guest appeared – a young man who had just arrived by train, and who had no clothes other than the scruffy and travel-stained ones he was wearing. Mortified by his faux pas, he had just joined the others when Rhodes came into the room – wearing a disreputable old blue suit.

His servants had told him what had happened, and he had changed out of his dinner jacket in order to welcome his guests.

Deciding on a menu

Everyone has heard of the vast banquets of imperial Rome; of the grilled peacocks and roast ostriches; of the dormice dipped in honey and the slaves pouring wine from huge jars; and of the gluttonous patricians stuffing themselves until they vomited, and then stuffing themselves some more.

But as the lawyer, observer and inveterate letter-writer Pliny the Younger reminds us, it wasn't always like that.

In a letter to a young friend, Junius Avitus, a rising young politician to whom Pliny was a moral guide and mentor, he described his disgust at being entertained by a man who claimed to have found the best way to combine splendour with economy. He and Pliny had the best of everything; there was cheaper food and wine for the bulk of the guests and an even lower grade of provisions for the former slaves who were there with their masters.

Pliny was outraged by what he called 'this conjunction of self indulgence and meanness'. At his own dinners, all the guests were fed the same, he said. 'Every man whom I have treated as equal with myself by inviting him to dinner, I treat as an equal in every way,' he said.

'What?' asked his host, incredulously. 'Even the former slaves?'

'Even the former slaves,' said Pliny. 'On occasions like that, I see them as my guests and companions.'

The other man laughed, still not believing him. 'That must put you to huge expense,' he objected. But Pliny shook his head. 'Not at all. My guests and former slaves do not drink wine that I normally do – I drink the same wine that they do.'

This, said Pliny, was a lesson that young Avitus should bear in mind. If a man is wise enough to curb his own greed, he will not find it so very expensive to entertain his visitors as he does himself.

Maybe to twenty-first-century ears, he might occasionally sound a bit of a self-satisfied and prosy old bore – but it's not bad advice, all the same.

How to escape a bore ...

One of the most common problems at a party is dealing with the person who just won't go away; the one who tells you the same story for a second or third time, the one who gets you in a corner and won't let you go, or the one who thinks that a conversation is carried on only with the mouth and not the ears as well. It's a problem that has probably existed for as long as people have talked to each other, and no one has come up with the perfect answer. But these three stories do at least show some of the ways people have tried to deal with it without being rude.

The poet Samuel Taylor Coleridge seems to have been, to put it politely, a difficult man to listen to. He, from time to time, used to give sermons at chapel services, and on one occasion asked his friend Charles Lamb whether he had heard him preach. 'My dear chap,' Lamb replied, 'I never heard you do anything else.'

Lamb also described how later – and maybe more kindly – he dealt with Coleridge's habit of holding him by the button of his coat and then, eyes closed and making languid gestures with his hand, starting on a rambling monologue that could sometimes go on for hours at a time:

I saw that it was no use to break away, so ... with my penknife I quietly severed the button from my coat and decamped. Five hours later and passing the same garden on my way home, I heard Coleridge's voice and, looking in, there he was with closed eyes, the button in his fingers, and his right hand gently waving, just as when I left him.

The great Victorian actor Henry Irving suffered a rather more forceful rebuff. Chatting to Mark Twain, he embarked on a lengthy story, but paused after a few sentences to ask if Twain had heard it before. 'No, no,' said Twain. 'Definitely not.' Irving resumed the tale, and then, a few moments later, broke off again.

'Are you quite sure you haven't heard this earlier?'

'No,' said Twain, slightly more testily, and off Irving went again. This time, he had almost reached the climax of the story before he paused to ask the same question. It was too much for Twain. 'I can lie once,' he said. 'I can lie twice for courtesy's sake, but I draw the line there. I can't lie for a third time at any price. And anyway, I invented the story!'

Again, that may be of limited use as a guide to how one should behave. But the poet Robert Browning had a technique that anyone could copy to this day. Tried beyond endurance at a party by a bore who showed no signs of letting him escape, he gave him his most engaging smile. 'But my dear fellow,' he said, patting him on the elbow, 'this is too bad of me. I'm monopolising you.'

And off he went, free at last, and no unpleasantness caused. A lesson to us all.

...And how not to do it

Winston Churchill's son, Randolph, was sometimes said to have inherited his father's irascibility but none of his charm. Unsurprisingly perhaps, he provides an example of how *not* to get rid of a monopolising bore with style.

He is said to have been buttonholed late at night, as he tried to leave his club, by a fellow member who was well known for his long and tedious stories. Randolph listened for as long as his patience lasted – probably not very long – and then called over one of the club's servants.

'Listen to his Lordship's story until he has finished,' he said, and left.

The bulldog & the chicken

Sir Winston Churchill, like Oscar Wilde and George Bernard Shaw, is a man around whom stories gather. Many of them are about his biting wit or his growling surliness. When France's President Charles de Gaulle, for instance – with whom he was never the best of friends – told him that the French people saw him as the reincarnation of Joan of Arc, Churchill reminded him with a harrumph: 'We had to burn the last one!'

But the old bulldog could also be as charming as a puppy. Being served with cold chicken at a rather refined buffet in America, he asked his hostess, 'May I have some breast, please?'

Slightly taken aback, she replied: 'Mr Prime Minister, in this country, we usually ask for white meat or dark meat.'

Churchill – who was, of course, half American – apologised profusely, and the next day the lady received an orchid brought by a personal courier. With it was a note from the British Prime Minister: 'I would be honoured if you would pin this on your white meat.'

The prime minister's pyjamas

It is practically an article of faith today that 'the old days' were a quieter, gentler time, when people treated each other more kindly and the world – or at least part of it – was cushioned in courtesy and consideration. So here is a story that seems to prove it.

It's set among the glittering young things that Evelyn Waugh wrote about in his novels – indeed, he used this incident as the basis for a scene in his book *Vile Bodies*.

Two young aristocratic sisters, Lady Sibell and Lady Mary Lygon, aged 22 and 19, and daughters of the immensely wealthy Lord Beauchamp, had spent the night partying in their white Norman Hartnell dresses. Then, like many young people before and since, they arrived home in the small hours to find themselves locked out. The doors of their father's Belgrave Square house were bolted, and the night footman – admittedly not a feature of most families – could not be woken.

So what could be more natural than that they should turn to an old family friend to ask for a bed for the night, or what was left of it? They hurried round to the friend's house, which was nearby, and summoned the night porter. He in turn called his master and mistress; and the Prime Minister of the United Kingdom, Right Honourable Stanley Baldwin, KG, PC, and his wife Lucy appeared in the hallway of 10 Downing Street in their nightclothes – Baldwin sporting a fetching pair of striped silk pyjamas beneath his dressing gown.

Of course the girls would be made welcome, Baldwin smiled courteously, and they were ushered off to their rooms. In the morning the prime minister made time to ring Lord Beauchamp – no doubt urging him not to be too cross with his wayward daughters – and asked him to send a maid round with some ordinary clothes for them. 'Balderdash and poppycock!' was the crusty old peer's reply; the girls had to walk home through the bustling streets of London in their full evening dress.

So far, so charming, even allowing for the fact that this little adventure took place in a world to which the vast mass of people had no access. The story seems as quaint and dated as a sepia photograph, although in fact, it's not so distant as it appears – Lady Sibell died only in 2005, at the age of 98.

But it may be worth remembering that the old days could be every bit as vicious, scandalous and unforgiving as our own times. Lord Beauchamp ended his days exiled and in disgrace, after a homosexual scandal that reached right to the top of British society; the two carefree young girls were bitterly estranged from their parents; and Baldwin spent his old age criticised and reviled by a nation that was bitter about his pre-war support for the appeasement policy.

But the image of the prime minister in his pyjamas, standing with his wife at the door of 10 Downing Street to welcome two young girls who were stranded and in trouble, remains as a reminder of the simpler, more caring time that we like to believe used to be.

The first to enter & the last to leave

In early May 1897 horrified newspaper readers all over the world were faced with the details of a horrific fire in Paris' *rue Jean Goujon*, in which scores of people had died. The fire had raged through the city's Great Charity Bazaar in minutes, apparently after a curtain caught fire while a film was being shown. Roofs of blazing tar had collapsed on to the heads of the workers, the exhibitors and the high society patrons of the event as they tried to flee.

The exact number of dead has never been established – some contemporary estimates were as high as 200, among them some of the most glittering names in Parisian society. Baroness Elizabeth St Martin; the Comtesse St Perrier; Madame Flores, the wife of the Spanish consul; the

Marchioness de Gallifet – the list of dead echoing the invitation list to one of the capital's most exclusive events. The bazaar had been planned as a massive event at which members of the French aristocracy would raise money for charity, and it had been widely supported.

But the highest ranking name of all was that of Sophie Charlotte, Duchesse d'Alençon, the sister of the Empress of Austria and the Queen of Sicily. The newspapers revealed that her engagement ring, inscribed with her name and that of her husband had been found; so had a silver watch, attached to a gold brooch that she was known to have been wearing. It was several days before her badly burned body was found.

Fireman, ordinary workmen, servants and tradesmen died in the blaze alongside the aristocrats – and struggled alongside them, too, to bring people out of the flames to safety. There were many tales of heroism that day, some of them tragic like the father who pulled his wife from the flames and then died with his daughter in his arms as he struggled to carry her to safety too. Some of them had happy endings. But it was only a few days later that the story of the death of the Duchesse d'Alençon began to emerge.

A group of workmen from a nearby site had fought their way through the flames to where the duchess' stall had been, at the far end of the bazaar. They had tried to persuade her to let them take her to safety on a nearby patch of waste ground, but she had refused; the girls who had been working with her on the charity stalls should be rescued first, she said.

'Because of my position, I was the first person to enter here,' she told them. 'Because of my position, I shall be the last to leave.'

A harsh lesson

There are, it seems, exceptions to the rule about making your guests feel at home. Some sins appear to be just too heinous to overlook. Take the grand society lady who saw, to her horror, that a young girl had lit a cigarette as the soup course was being cleared away. With a melodramatic clearing of her throat, and a stare that would have stripped paint at 30 yards, she rose to her feet.

'We appear to have finished,' she said in a ringing voice, and led her guests from the room.

Dinner was over – and the mortified young girl probably never smoked during a meal again.

An old-fashioned way of business

Since its foundation in the eighteenth century, Coutts and Company has enjoyed an unrivalled reputation as the bank of high society, offering its services to the queen and generations of the royal family. This relationship began in the 1760s, when George III opened an account with Thomas Coutts, one of the two Scottish brothers who founded the bank.

Coutts had been dining with some of his fellow financiers, and heard one of them telling a story about refusing a loan to a certain nobleman who needed £30,000 – something over £2 million in today's money. Coutts said nothing, but later that night went to the peer's house and left a message to say that if his lordship were to call the following morning, he might learn something to his advantage.

Intrigued, the nobleman was ushered into Coutts' offices the next day. The banker took a bundle of banknotes from a drawer, and counted out £31,000 on his desk. 'I believe this is what you require,' he said. Astonished, the peer asked what security would be required for the loan. 'I shall be more than satisfied with your lordship's note of hand,' Coutts replied.

This may not be a style of banking that would be acceptable these days, but it resulted in the peer opening a large account with Coutts' bank shortly afterwards, when he sold an estate – and also led to his recommending the bank a short while later to King George.

Family embarrassment

A wise man once said that a good host should make his guests feel at home even when he wishes that they were – but for the queen, the problem is sometimes quite the reverse. She has to make her hosts feel at ease, even when they are the president and First Lady of the United States.

In November 1985 President Gerald Ford and his wife Betty entertained the queen and Prince Philip to dinner. Their 23-year-old son, Jack, was dressing for the formal introductions when he realised that he had lost the studs for his dress shirt. He just had time to rush to his father's room to borrow some, and so shirt unfastened, hair tousled, and in his stockinged feet, he dashed down the corridor and into the lift – to find his parents with their royal guests already there.

Mrs Ford began to introduce her son and apologise for his appearance, but the queen stopped her. 'I have one at home just like that,' she smiled.

❧

A noble restraint

In his diaries, the British theatre critic James Agate (1877– 1947) recalled lunching with a duke at the latter's house in London in the 1930s. A well-known and much admired film actress of the day had also been invited. One o'clock arrived, and there was still no sign of the actress; nor had she arrived an hour later, by which time small talk was flagging and everyone was probably pie-eyed on sherry. Eventually, at 2.30 p.m., the butler answered the door to admit, in a cloud of 'Darlings!', the tardy guest, followed by her maid, who was struggling beneath a pile of packages and boxes.

Rushing to kiss the duke, the new arrival said breathlessly, 'Darling! I am *so* sorry if I'm just the teeniest bit late, but I simply *had* to buy a chandelier!'

At which the duke, detaching himself from her embrace, fixed his gaze on the ceiling and said quietly to himself, 'I once knew a chap who bought a chandelier *after* luncheon ...'

A fine line

For visitors to the houses of the rich, famous and aristocratic, there is often a fine line to be drawn between courtesy and abject sycophancy. During the nineteenth century the wealthy landowner Lord Crewe had his palatial home, Crewe Hall in Cheshire, extensively rebuilt after a fire. Part of the £150,000 project – worth some £10 million at today's rates – was the reconstruction of a magnificent carved Jacobean staircase which swept down into the central hall.

He was known to be justifiably proud of his house, and particularly of his staircase – so when an elderly lady who was visiting slipped on the top step and tumbled the full length of the stairs, there was considerable consternation.

As she lay stunned at the foot of the carved and gilded oak newel posts, her husband dashed forward to speak to his lordship. 'Oh, Lord Crewe,' he said, 'I do hope my wife hasn't damaged your beautiful staircase.'

Putting a name to a face

During the 1920s Douglas Fairbanks' Beverly Hills mansion, Pickfair, was the acknowledged centre of Hollywood social life. Apart from a glittering array of film stars and writers, guests at the parties given by Fairbanks and his wife Mary Pickford included a number of the crowned heads of Europe and several members of the English aristocracy.

One day, Fairbanks was driving home when he saw a figure he vaguely recognised walking along the road in the heat. He stopped the car to offer the man a lift, registering his cut-glass English accent, expensively styled suit and aristocratic bearing – but still struggling to put a name to the face.

As they drove along they chatted about the challenges of owning and maintaining a twenty-two room mansion, with its fabulous art collection and its extensive grounds, and Fairbanks' passenger made several incisive and approving comments about the organisation of the whole Pickfair estate. Clearly, he was accustomed to living in some style; he must, Fairbanks concluded, be one of his recent aristocratic guests.

Still unwilling to face the embarrassment of admitting that he could not remember his friend's name, he invited him in for a drink, and snatched the opportunity of asking his secretary what the man was called. 'He's obviously a lord, but I can't remember his name,' he said.

'Don't know the guy's name, Mr Fairbanks,' came the laconic reply. 'But he's the English butler you fired last month for drunkenness.'

⤫

A marriage proposal

During the First World War, the Buckinghamshire estate of Cliveden – later notorious as the stately home at the heart of the Profumo scandal – was used as a Red Cross hospital for wounded soldiers from the trenches.

Cliveden's chatelaine Nancy Astor, American-born wife of Viscount Astor, was then in her mid-thirties, and worked among the soldiers as a nurse, tending their wounds. One day a young Canadian soldier, who had been lying unconscious, awoke to find her gazing down at him. Entranced by her beauty, he murmured: 'You're the kind of person I'd like to take back to Canada as my wife.' (Being a soldier, he may well have made other suggestions as well, but whoever passed on the original story limited them to this tentative proposal of marriage.)

Viscountess Astor smiled down at him. 'Let me think it over for a day or so,' she said.

A few days later, one of the other patients told the rapidly recovering soldier the name of the nurse he had flirted with. The next time he saw her, he apologised abjectly, covered in confusion.

Her response? 'I haven't had such a compliment for a long time!'

Invitation to dinner

A truly generous host will ignore the rudeness of his guest, and make him feel at home however bad his behaviour has been – but courtesy is not always what it seems. This cautionary tale is told by the Victorian painter, W.P. Frith, in his autobiography.

Frith says that a distant cousin of his made a bet that he would gain entrance to the famously beautiful private gardens at Fonthill Abbey, the Wiltshire home of the writer William Beckford. Beckford, author of the gothic horror novel *Vathek*, was reputed to be a surly recluse who would not tolerate intrusions on his privacy.

Frith's cousin slipped into the park at Fonthill, through a gate that had been carelessly left open in the high stone walls that surrounded it, and was leaning on the second wall that separated the park from the abbey gardens when he was approached by a gardener. Far from throwing him out, the gardener offered to give him a tour of the grounds – and then, astonishingly, invited the young intruder into the abbey itself to look at Mr Beckford's fabled collections of books and paintings. Finally, seeing it was late in the afternoon, he insisted that he should stay for dinner – and when the young man demurred, the gardener declared that he was William Beckford himself.

The food and drink were magnificent, and Beckford's conversation fascinating. His guest hung on every word of his stories of Italian travel; his meetings with aristocrats, writers and artists; his philosophical thoughts; and his views on art and music. Surely, he thought, Beckford's reputation as a man who hated company was a gross libel.

And then, on the stroke of eleven, the famous author got up and left the room. The young man waited for him to return ... and waited. He must have dozed off, because he was suddenly aware of the footman putting out the lights. Mr Beckford, the footman told him as he led him to the great oak front door, had gone to bed.

'This is very strange,' he said. 'I expected Mr Beckford back again. I wished to thank him for his hospitality.'

'Mr Beckford ordered me to present his compliments to you, sir,' replied the footman. 'I am to say that as you found your way into Fonthill Abbey without permission, you may find your way out again as best you can. And he hopes you will take care to avoid the bloodhounds that are let loose in the garden every night.'

And with that the door slammed shut. Hearing the baying of the bloodhounds, the young man climbed the first tree he could find and spent a long and miserable night there until daybreak when he escaped. He had won his bet – but, he said, 'not for fifty million times the amount would I again pass such a night as I did at Fonthill Abbey.'

7

SPORTING GESTURES

Any dedicated sportsman will tell you that there's no point in playing the game if you don't play to win. Nice guys, they say, always come last – and there are plenty of stories to show that gamesmanship, cheating and unsportsmanlike behaviour can be effective. But as long as sport has been played, there have also been people who have wanted to win, but not at any price. The tradition of courtesy and generosity in sport is a long and honourable one, and these stories demonstrate that it knows no distinction between gentlemen and players, or between amateurs and professionals. Whether they are amateur athletes from a bygone age, or Premiership footballers in our own time, there are dedicated competitors who clearly believe that there are some things – not many of them, perhaps, but still some things – that are more important than winning. And the strange thing is they often do win in the end. Nice guys, in fact, do sometimes come first.

Walking the walk

Adam Gilchrist, wicket-keeper batsman for the Australian cricket team until 2008, was an unusual cricketer. It's not just that he played international cricket for twelve years, and not even that he's generally considered to have been one of the best wicket-keepers in history.

Gilchrist used to walk.

That means that when he was batting, if he knew he'd nicked the ball to the wicket-keeper, he would set off for the pavilion without waiting for the umpire to make a decision. Walking is a sporting admission by a batsman that he's out that's often seen as the mark of a gentleman in cricket – and it is increasingly rare in the international game. Most batsmen stand their ground and thank their lucky stars if the umpire makes a mistake in their favour.

In his book *Walking to Victory*, Gilchrist described a World Cup semi-final match against Sri Lanka in 2003 where he knew he'd given a thick edge to the wicket-keeper. The Sri Lankans appealed, but the umpire shook his head, meaning that he didn't think Gilchrist had touched the ball, and so was not out.

But Gilchrist knew better. 'The voice in my head was emphatic. Go. Walk. And I did,' he said:

Of course, the guys back in the viewing room were a bit stunned at what I'd done. Flabbergasted, really, that I'd do it in a World Cup semi. While I sat there, thinking about it and being asked about it, I kept going back to the fact that, well, at the end of the day, I had been honest with myself. I felt it was time that players made a stand to take back responsibility for the game.

Walking isn't just a demonstration of sportsmanship and honesty – it's an act of courtesy to the opposing team, and especially to the umpire. After his action in the Sri Lanka match, Gilchrist says, he was worried that he might have embarrassed umpire Rudi Koertzen, who had initially given him not out – but when he caught his eye as the teams took the field at the beginning of the next innings, Koertzen gave a little nod and a brief clap of his hands in silent appreciation of what he'd done.

None of this means that Gilchrist is pious or self-satisfied. Asked some years later whether he would walk if he nicked a ball to the wicket-keeper in the final Test Match of a series, with Australia needing a few runs to win and just one wicket left, he paused, puffed out his cheeks, and gave the question a moment's thought.

'Ah, mate,' he said. 'In those circumstances, I wouldn't be nicking the ball behind in the first place.'

A true champion

Courtesy is what makes the cliché true: sport really can be less about winning and more about taking part. Matthew Syed, once an international table tennis player and now a respected sports journalist, tells a story about the greatest victory of his sporting career, against the then world champion, Jörgen Persson of Sweden.

It was the tense climax of a hard-fought match, he said in his column in *The Times*. The score was 19–19 in the deciding fifth game – with both players trying to qualify for the 1996 Olympics – and then, one of Syed's shots seemed to miss the end of the table. Point to Persson.

But what Persson had seen was that the ball had actually grazed the edge of the table, only by a whisker, but enough to mean that the point should have been Syed's. No one else had seen it; not umpires, not spectators and certainly not Syed.

The stakes could not have been higher, and there could have been no one to blame Persson if he had simply kept quiet and taken the point and probably won the game, and hence the match.

'Persson did not hesitate, not for an instant, nodding in my direction, signalling what had happened and turning the scoreboard in my favour,' says Syed:

I was so surprised, so touched, that I said something that still echoes in my ears today: 'Are you sure?'

'Yes, I am sure,' he said.

Afterwards, having won the match, I approached Persson and thanked him for his integrity. 'I wanted to win,' he said. 'But not if it meant winning like that.'

The greatest sporting encounters ever?

It is possible to see the history of polar exploration as one of scientific advance, or even as part of the imperialism with which western nations seized great tracts of the world for themselves. But occasionally, the polar adventure was a straightforward race between rival expeditions; and it was always a contest between brave men and the elements. Maybe the journeys to the North and South Poles have been, in essence, a series of the greatest sporting encounters ever.

There have been stories of incredible achievement, such as that of the Norwegian explorer Roald Amundsen, who won the race against Robert Falcon Scott's British expedition in January 1912. Scott himself told a story of tragedy and nobility, with his account of the self sacrifice of Captain Lawrence Oates, who famously walked to his death in a polar storm rather than slow down his colleagues in their doomed attempt to reach safety. Oates' memorial, erected near the scene of his death by the rescuers who eventually found the bodies of his companions, described him as 'a very gallant gentleman'. His reported last words, 'I am just going outside, and I may be some time', exemplified the sense of chivalry and self-effacement implicit in that description.

And Scott's own words, left in his journal as he lay dying in his tent, also deserve to be remembered for their dignity: 'We took risks, we knew we took them; things have come out against us, and therefore we have no cause for complaint, but bow to the will of Providence, determined still to do our best to the last.'

But there has also been comedy in the frozen wastes of the Antarctic. Sir Edgeworth David was a distinguished Australian geologist who accompanied the explorer Ernest Shackleton on the expedition of 1907–09, which travelled further south than anyone had managed before. During the expedition Shackleton's physicist, Douglas Mawson, was working in his tent when he heard a cry from outside. It was Sir Edgeworth.

'Are you very busy?' he called.

Mawson, who was correlating some data and did not want to be disturbed, replied rather testily, 'Yes, I am. What is it?'

There was a pause. 'Are you really *very* busy?' came the call.

'Yes, actually,' Mawson snapped back. It is seldom a good idea to interrupt a physicist while he is working on his data. 'What is it that you want?'

There was another short pause, and then the impeccably mannered Sir Edgeworth shouted back apologetically, 'Well, it's just that I'm down a crevasse, and I'm not sure that I can hang on much longer!'

How things can be

It's more than seventy years since he won his four Olympic gold medals and more than thirty years since he died, but Jesse Owens remains one of the most evocative names in Olympic history. His triumphs in the 1936 Berlin Games – where he won gold medals in the 100 metres, the 200 metres, the long jump and the 100-metre relay – challenged the unshakable belief of his Nazi hosts in the superiority of white men over black, angered Hitler and delighted most of the rest of the world.

Enough went on in public to justify the respect and fame that his name still enjoys – although in the years immediately following his triumph he went home to face a climate of racial prejudice in the US, eke out a living as a petrol pump attendant and eventually file for bankruptcy. But in private, Owens' long jump victory was the setting for an inspirational story of sportsmanship and human decency that transcended Nazi ideology.

Owens was competing against a blonde German hero, Carl Ludwig 'Luz' Long, who was widely expected to take the gold. During the competition, the two struck up a friendship that lasted for years. Some unconfirmed reports suggest that Long even helped his rival by marking the right take-off point for him when Owens, facing possible elimination from the competition, had to take a crucial qualifying jump. That may or may not be true – but what is known is that, after Owens' victory, when Hitler had stormed out of the stadium rather than present the gold medal to a black runner, Long, the silver medalist, was the first to offer his congratulations.

'It took a lot of courage for him to befriend me in front of Hitler. You can melt down all the medals and cups I have, and there wouldn't be a plating on the 24 carat friendship I felt for Luz Long at that moment,' Owens told reporters afterwards.

Because of the war the two men never met again, but they exchanged letters. Seven years later, Long – not a member of the Nazi Party, but a soldier in the German army – wrote to his old rival:

> My heart tells me this will be the last letter I write … If it is so, I ask you something. It is for you to go to Germany when this war is done, someday find my son and tell him about his father. Tell him, Jesse, what times were like when we were not separated by war … I am saying, tell him how things can be between men on this earth.

It was Long's last letter. Shortly afterwards he was killed during the German invasion of Sicily. Owens not only fulfilled his request, and maintained a regular correspondence with Long's son Kai, but also stood by Kai's side in the 1960s as best man at his wedding. He did indeed tell him, and a whole generation, how things can be between men on this earth.

No dumbbells here

Bear Bryant was a famous American college football coach during the fifties, sixties and seventies, who was noted for his tough, no-nonsense approach towards his players. One of the stars who played for him – 'the greatest athlete I ever coached,' Bryant said – was the great quarterback Joe Namath.

The coach was a strict disciplinarian, the player known for speaking his mind: it could have been a recipe for conflict. Instead, it showed that courtesy and affection aren't necessarily incompatible with a sense of humour.

On one occasion, Bryant was growling at his University of Alabama squad about the need for self-respect on and off the field. 'This is a class operation. I want your shoes to be shined, I want you to have a tie on, to get your hair cut, and to keep a crease in your pants. I also want you to go to class,' he said. 'I don't want no dumbbells on this team. If there is a dumbbell in this room, I want him to stand up.'

Nobody moved. You just didn't take on Bear Bryant in that way. Then, slowly and deliberately, Namath rose to his feet.

Bryant looked at him in surprise for a second. 'Joe, how come you're standing up? You ain't dumb.'

'Well,' said Namath, 'it's just that I hate like the devil to see you standing up there all by yourself, Coach.'

The right thing to do

Paulo di Canio, the Italian football star who played in the English Premiership from 1997 to 2004, is nobody's idea of a pussycat. In 1998, for instance, he served an eleven-match suspension for pushing over the referee who sent him off while playing for Sheffield Wednesday against Arsenal.

And yet, among professional footballers, his name is forever linked with one of the most striking displays of instinctive sportsmanship seen in the modern game.

In December 2000, di Canio was playing for West Ham against Everton. The match was well into injury time, with the teams level at one goal all, when a cross came over from the right wing to di Canio, waiting in the Everton penalty area. There was an open goal; all he had to do was bring the ball down and put it in the net, and his team would take the valuable three points for a win away from home.

Instead, he caught the ball in his arms, conceding an automatic free kick, and gesturing towards the Everton goalkeeper, Paul Gerrard, lying in agony on the ground several yards away. In fact, Gerrard had twisted his knee, but di Canio believed he could have broken his leg. It was more important, he thought, that his fellow professional should get urgent medical attention than that he should score the winning goal.

'I saw the goalkeeper doubled over. I saw his knee twisted in the wrong direction,' he said. 'It seemed like the right thing to do, but I didn't really think about it. A serious injury to any professional is far worse than losing two points.'

The Everton crowd gave di Canio an immediate standing ovation; his manager, Harry Redknapp, described the incident as 'sportsmanship of the highest merit'; FIFA, football's international governing body, presented him with its special Fair Play Award. But the player himself was bemused by all the attention he achieved.

'I am not a saint, just like I was not a killer two years ago with the referee when I did something wrong,' he said. 'During the game, the opposition is my enemy. But when they are injured, they are my colleagues and I must help them.'

Sports fans who want to be grumpy might say that the fact that such an act of sportsmanship should have received so much attention simply shows how low standards usually are. But di Canio's own words – 'It seemed like the right thing to do, but I didn't really think about it' – surely sum up something very important about the way sport should be played.

❧

A great Olympian

There's no reason why the courtesy of great sportsmen should be extended only to their competitors; no reason, in fact, why courtesy should be extended only to human beings. Take the case of the great Australian Olympian Bobby Pearce – Henry Robert Pearce, to give him his full name. Pearce was an oarsman who won gold in the single sculls event at the 1928 Amsterdam Olympics, and successfully defended his title four years later in Los Angeles, going on later in his career to become World Champion from 1933 to 1938.

In Amsterdam, Pearce stormed through his heats on the city's Stoten Canal, beating the opposition with several lengths to spare. In the quarter final, the same pattern seemed to be repeating itself, with Pearce building up a commanding lead over his French opponent Victor Saurin.

But then, glancing over his shoulder, he saw a mother duck with a small train of ducklings behind her swimming directly into his path. Pearce leant on his oars, bringing his boat to a shuddering stop as the family of ducks passed serenely in front of him. Saurin, meanwhile, who had no idea what had happened, caught up with him and powered past, pulling away to a lead of five lengths. But with the ducks safely out of the way, Pearce started rowing again and won the race, going on through the semi-final and the final to take the gold with a new Olympic record – surely one of the most unusual victories in Olympic history.

Count me out

On 14 May 1938 the England football team played Germany at Berlin's *Olympiastadion*. Was it, as several newspapers have suggested, the most shameful moment in British sporting history? Or was it simply the members of a national team showing courtesy and civility towards their hosts?

Britain's ambassador to Germany, Sir Neville Henderson, had no doubts when he advised the team on how they should behave. 'When I go to see Herr Hitler, I give him the Nazi salute, because that is the normal courtesy expected,' he said. The Football Association officials with the team agreed – and that is how photographs came to be taken of an England football team standing with their arms raised in the Nazi salute as the band played *Deutschland über alles*. Among them was possibly the country's greatest ever football hero, Sir Stanley Matthews.

In fact, Hitler was not at the match – but for some of the players, it was a defining moment. England's captain, the Arsenal fullback Eddie Hapgood, later served in the Royal Air Force. 'I've been V-bombed in Brussels before the Rhine crossing, and bombed and rocketed in London; I've been in a shipwreck, a train crash, and inches short of a plane accident,' he said later. 'But the worst moment of my life, and the one I would not willingly go through again, was giving the Nazi salute in Berlin.'

The Football Association secretary, Stanley Rous, couldn't see what the fuss was about. The players, he said, 'no doubt saw it as a bit of fun'.

In fact, at least one of them, even at the time, certainly didn't. Stan Cullis, one of the defensive line-up alongside Hapgood and the youngest member of the team at just 22, gave a brisk, no-nonsense reply to the idea of the salute. 'Count me out,' he said – and they did, dropping him from the team.

It was a great night for England, who thrashed Germany 6–3. But perhaps as Cullis got older – he was 85 when he died in 2001, after a long and honourable career at Wolverhampton as both player and manager – he would look back on that match as the international cap he was glad he never got.

Indeed, there may be ways to play with tyrants and make a point. In 1974 the British Lions rugby team set off on a controversial tour of apartheid South Africa. Some players who would have been in the party had stayed at home and opted not to go on the tour; some were there to see for themselves what apartheid meant; others on the tour believed sincerely that sport and politics should not mix. Some, perhaps, didn't care anyway.

But the South Africans, terrified at the prospect of international sporting boycotts, were delighted to see them. A television reporter, no doubt bearing in mind the stereotype of a rugby player as a hard drinking, hard partying knucklehead who liked nothing better than a good sing-song, asked on air what was the Lions' team song.

'It's a song by the Specials,' came the reply. 'It's called *Free Nelson Mandela*.'